JOINING THE CONVERSATION

PARISH LIFE SOURCEBOOKS

JOINING THE CONVERSATION

JESUS MATTHEW LUKE & US

BARBARA HALL

SERIES INTRODUCTION

JOHN B. COBURN

International Standard Book No.: 0-936384-25-5
Library of Congress Catalog No.: 84-72480

Cover design by James Madden, SSJE
Published in the United States of America by Cowley Publications
    980 Memorial Drive, Cambridge, MA 02138

to my parents
Clarence and Blanche Hall,
from whom I first heard the parables of Jesus,
with gratitude and love

SERIES INTRODUCTION

Parish Life Sourcebooks is a new series of books which address issues arising in the parish for lay persons as well as clergy. Sourcebooks from Cowley Publications not only suggest solutions to parish problems, they also create imaginative alternatives to traditionally accepted ways of thinking about a particular issue. Such issues—from new concepts in Bible study and issuing sacraments to children to the concerns of becoming a eucharistic parish—have a wide-ranging impact throughout the parish, and are the sort of questions that emerge at coffee hours where clergy and laity informally grapple with theological concerns.

Parish Life Sourcebooks are working documents designed to assist in these theological conversations. On the one hand each provides a presentation of an essential parish issue, covering the basic information needed for a full discussion; on the other, Cowley Sourcebooks serve as a springboard for dialogue, encouraging readers to go beyond the book itself to create their own interpretations of the issues and search for their own conclusions. Through wide margins, ample end pages, and helpful bibliographies, Sourcebooks lend themselves to the complete use of the reader, becoming, if used to their full potential, that reader's own creation.

Parish Life Sourcebooks assist each parish community, regardless of affiliation or denomination, in the effort to bring together clergy and laity on key issues that they face on a daily basis. In so far as Sourcebooks encourage healthy discussion on topics we do not often speak about, but on which we always have an opinion, we welcome them into the theological arena of our time.

The Society of St. John the Evangelist is continuing to produce for the Church attractive, intelligently prepared books that are consistent with the tradition of Cowley and related to the contemporary parish scene. They are, in my judgment, among the finest publications available for the Church at large. I am very happy to commend them to clergy and lay persons. They will provide interesting and stimulating materials for further theological reflection and prayer leading to a deeper and richer commitment to the Christian Gospel.

John B. Coburn
Bishop of Massachusetts

PREFACE

This book is designed for the use of anyone who has an interest in Jesus' teaching about the kingdom of God. For this reason I have avoided the technical language of New Testament study by specialists. Nevertheless I am indebted to many of those specialists who have been my teachers and colleagues in conversation about the teachings of Jesus. No one does this sort of work alone.

The book takes its point of departure from the Parable of the Great Feast, which has various titles in the different translations of the New Testament. The parable is found in Matthew 22:1-14 and Luke 14:15-24, and the translation used here is the Revised Standard Version.

This book is the product of the collaboration and help of a number of partners in conversation about the parable, to whom I am deeply grateful. They include Cynthia Shattuck, editor and valued colleague, J. Louis Martyn, who first suggested to me the notion that we are in conversation with the Bible and who continued to help me explore the idea, and Bruce Boston, longtime theological colleague, partner in dialogue, and friend. Of particular value has been the contribution of two friends who have walked and talked with me throughout the writing of this book, Moira Burnham and Diana MacVeagh.

Most of all I am indebted to those who have been my students, some of whose writing about the parable is included here. To them, and to others not represented here, I wish to express my profound thanks for all they have taught me and shared with me through the years.

Barbara Hall
General Theological Seminary

CONTENTS

Introduction   1

1. Jesus' Conversation with His
   Contemporaries   10

2. Matthew and Luke Join the Conversation   33

3. We Join the Conversation   68

   Bibliography   103

Introduction

There are many ways to read and use the Bible profitably, and the premise of this book is that all of these ways involve us in conversation. We do not come to the Bible with blank minds and hearts. When we come, we bring with us all the questions and problems, all the delights and joys, all the dilemmas and mysteries, all the sorrows and difficulties, all the ideas and convictions that make us the people we are. We also bring all the things we have learned and thought about the Bible previously, as well as a good deal of what the church has said about it. When we read it and work with it, we are in conversation with it. We speak to it as it speaks to us. This is true of historians who tend to believe their discipline is an 'objective' one. It is true of those who have absorbed the scientific, technological mentality of our times, the people who always ask whether something is 'literally' true. And it is the case of those who learned in childhood either that God is love, or that God is a fearsome tyrant, or both.

Conversation means we are not passive recipients of something imposed on us, but active participants in whatever happens when we come to the Bible. Yet we do not often recognize the fact that a conversation is taking place, and so it is the intention of this book to make the conversation audible and conscious.

In a conversation different voices are heard. Every voice does not say the same thing. Each of us has a stake in the talk; each one speaks and listens out of a particular context and situation. In a good conversation the different voices are not merged into one; rather, people listen to each other and learn from each other. A great deal can happen in a conversation; there may be a lot at stake. Lives can be changed.

Good conversation, real conversation, demands a lot from its participants in the way of discipline, openness, tolerance, and conviction. Most of all, good conversation demands imagination.

To listen to someone is to imagine ourselves in that person's shoes, to suspend for a moment our own preoccupations in order to enter imaginatively into another's life. This need for imagination is especially true when we are in conversation with people who are very different from us—people who come from a different background and culture, for example, people who speak a language other than our own, people who lived in another time.

What does it mean to read the gospels as conversation? It means first of all to understand that Jesus was in conversation with his own contemporaries. He spoke concretely to the people he addressed; he did not speak in an abstract, timeless way that would force his listeners to figure out how to 'apply' what he said to their own lives. Particularly in his parables, Jesus spoke about ordinary events and about things that were close to the daily lives of his hearers. If we read Jesus' words with no appreciation of the situation in which he first spoke them, his words lose their impact. We fail to hear his voice. For Jesus to tell us that 'God is love' does not help us. Our real need is to know in what way and under what circumstances 'God is love.' What does it mean when we are in danger or when our child is sick or when we are tired and lonely?

To listen to Jesus in conversation with his contemporaries is also to learn that he invited, provoked, demanded a response from them. This was especially the case when he taught them in parables. It was precisely the purpose of these parables to stir people up, cause them to question their normal ideas about things, crack open the smooth surface of their prejudices and the compromises they had made in order to get on with life. Jesus did not tell pat little morality stories; he dropped bombshells into people's lives. His listeners could turn away and leave, shutting out his voice; what they could not do was remain with him as passive listeners. Jesus called them into engagement with himself and with their own lives. He offered them power to live. He can do the same for us if we enter into real conversation with him, if we take up the challenge he offers.

When Jesus' earliest followers told, retold, preserved, and finally wrote down the stories about him, they were joining a conversation both with him and with their own contemporaries. They had been gripped by the conviction that in the life, death, and resurrection of Jesus and in the subsequent pouring out of the Holy Spirit upon his followers, God was doing something truly radical and drastic about the world. The church was not founded on Jesus' teachings, but on the astonishing conviction that this one who had walked among them was God's Messiah, the one God sent to save the world and its inhabitants from themselves and from sin, the one through whom it was now possible to live in this world with God. Those who told and preserved the stories about Jesus' ministry were the same people whose lives had been turned upside down and given new direction by God's action in Jesus Christ. It would be astonishing indeed if this amazing turn of events had made no impression at all on their memories of Jesus.

And so they became the earliest church. Those who told and preserved the stories about Jesus which we have in our gospels were in a brand new situation. They knew themselves to be called by God to proclaim the message of Jesus Christ. In using the stories about Jesus for that purpose, they took part in a double conversation. They were in conversation with Jesus, responding to his challenge, but they were also in conversation with their contemporaries, just as Jesus had been with his. Their primary motive in telling and preserving these stories was not to keep an accurate record of what Jesus had said and done. They were not first of all archivists. What they wanted to do was much more important. Their primary purpose was to use the stories as powerful vehicles for their proclamation, just as Jesus in his time had used the same stories as powerful vehicles for his message.

What was the result of this double conversation? The stories Jesus told began to undergo changes as they were retold by his followers. His parables were adapted and interpreted in order that they might continue to speak powerfully in a new situation. Two versions of the Parable of the Great Feast, the focus of this book, have come down to us. Each is very different from the other because they address two very different sets of people. At the

4

same time, study of these two versions of the same story turns up the surprising fact that the original story has not been obliterated in the changing of it. Both Matthew and Luke have left clues that help us discern the original parable they received and changed. It is as if they were inviting us to do a little work of our own on the parable, work that we will do in the following pages. For the moment, we register the intriguing fact that our gospel writers appear both to have a great respect for and at the same time enjoy a great freedom in relation to the parable they received.

If Matthew and Luke are free to change the parable, are we free to do the same? When we read it, we too are invited to join the conversation. We can listen to all the voices speaking to us in this parable, which include not only Jesus' voice but also Matthew's and Luke's, and attempt to appreciate the circumstances and the people they are speaking to. And we can also speak in and to our circumstances; we have questions of our own to ask. Our telling of the parable will address issues important to us and to our contemporaries, some of which are different from those raised by Jesus and his earlier followers. We hope that when we do this the parable, powerful in other times, will become powerful for us today.

Because we can discern more than one voice in the conversation, there is no one right way to tell the parable. Matthew and Luke exercised their imaginations as they retold the parable, just as Jesus had done when he created it. We are invited to do the same. The product of our imagination is not a new right answer, but an offering. Someone else, doing the same work that we will undertake in the following pages, would speak differently. That is cause for rejoicing. What each of us says to everyone else in the conversation is: does it help us to tell the story this way?

We will work on the Parable of the Great Feast for a number of reasons. First, Jesus uses the parable to speak, as he so often does, about the kingdom of God. It is a central theme in his ministry. Another reason for choosing this parable lies in its length; it is a story with plot, characters, and narrative development. Consequently it offers scope for some serious analysis.

Still a third reason is the fact that the parable contains some anomalies, some puzzles. The conversation will be much more interesting if we have a few tough problems to work on.

My major reason for choosing this parable, however, is that it has stimulated diverse and imaginative responses from some of my students taking part in a course on the New Testament. Some of these responses are found in the last chapter of this book. Their contributions to the ongoing conversation brought the parable alive in ways that first suggested to me that this book might be worth doing.

The methods that will allow us to hear the different voices in the conversation are those normally used by specialists in New Testament study, but little used outside that limited circle. While the specialist has information at her disposal not readily available elsewhere, there is no reason why others cannot use the methods with profit. The work involved requires some discipline and the use of a few resources, but anyone can join the conversation.

Careful study suggests that there are a number of layers of tradition we can discern in the gospels. These are

1) Jesus' own words and actions;
2) the earliest telling and retelling of the stories of Jesus;
3) the beginnings of written collections of stories about Jesus;
4) the gospels.

In discussing the Parable of the Great Feast we will attempt to reconstruct these layers, beginning with the fourth and latest: the versions we have in Matthew and Luke. Then we will search for a possible source of the parable that these two writers shared, to put ourselves in touch with the third layer—the written collections of stories about Jesus. Next, we will test this reconstructed source to see whether it recorded the parable as it was told orally, in order to put ourselves in touch with the second layer of tradition, the earliest telling and retelling of the stories about Jesus. Then we will test the oral version to see if Jesus told the parable in this form, which will put us in touch with the earliest layer of tradition, that is, Jesus' own words.

These three steps constitute the first chapter of the book. At each stage in the life of the parable we will ask what issues were at stake for those who told (or wrote) and heard the parable. The chapter concludes with our attempt to hear the parable as Jesus' original listeners heard it.

In chapter two we will return to the reconstructed source received by Matthew and Luke and ask what the gospel writers have done to the parable, and why. We will try to listen to their versions as their original readers did.

In chapter three, we will try to join the conversation ourselves and look at some contemporary responses to the parable. As readers, you are encouraged to participate. It is best to read Matthew's and Luke's versions of the parable at the beginning of the first chapter and note your own reactions then, before going on to read the chapter. When it is time to join the conversation, you can review your earlier reactions in order to make certain that these concerns become part of the conversation. It is hoped that this book will be studied and discussed in groups. Conversation with our own contemporaries will greatly add to the richness and diversity of the conversation with Jesus, Matthew, and Luke.

The major purpose of the book is to enter into conversation with Jesus and some of his early followers about the kingdom of God. The kingdom is not an easy subject to discuss. Usually we settle for the notion that the kingdom is either an interior reality, hidden in each one of us, or a future reality for which we have to wait. In neither case does the kingdom of God seem to make a significant impact on the way we live our daily lives. So we hope to be challenged in this belief by some surprises from Jesus, and from Matthew and Luke.

A second purpose of the book is to demonstrate a few of the methods that can help us to hear the voices of Jesus and some of his followers in their own situations. Because these methods are not well known or much used by lay people, we will concentrate on one parable rather than attempting to work on many. The same methods described here can also be used to uncover voices in the conversation in any other gospel passage. In working on only one parable, we will keep in mind that a single story does not say everything. Our aim will be to discover what it does say.

Matthew and Luke, in conversation with Jesus and with their own contemporaries, transformed the parable that Jesus told—

each in his own way. When we join the conversation, perhaps we will find that we need to transform the parable still further in order for it to speak with power in our own day as it did in Jesus' and Matthew's and Luke's. It is to be hoped that in the process of the conversation, we will discover that the parable is transforming us.

THE PARABLE OF THE GREAT FEAST —
MATTHEW'S VERSION
Mt 22:1-14

22: 1 And again Jesus spoke to them in parables, saying,
2 "The kingdom of heaven may be compared to a king who
gave a marriage feast for his son, 3 and sent his servants to call
those who were invited to the marriage feast, but they would not
come. 4 Again he sent other servants, saying, 'Tell those who are
invited, Behold I have made ready my dinner, my oxen and my
fat calves are killed, and everything is ready; come to the marriage
feast.' 5 But they made light of it and went off, one to his farm,
another to his business, 6 while the rest seized his servants,
treated them shamefully, and killed them. 7 The king was angry,
and he sent his troops and destroyed those murderers and burned
their city. 8 Then he said to his servants, 'The wedding is ready,
but those invited were not worthy. 9 Go therefore to the
thoroughfares, and invite to the marriage feast as many as you
find.' 10 And those servants went out into the streets and
gathered all whom they found, both bad and good; so the wedding
hall was filled with guests.
    11 But when the king came in to look at the guests, he saw
there a man who had no wedding garment; 12 and he said to him,
'Friend, how did you get in here without a wedding garment?'
And he was speechless. 13 Then the king said to the attendants,
'Bind him hand and foot, and cast him into the outer darkness;
there men will weep and gnash their teeth.' 14 For many are
called, but few are chosen."

THE PARABLE OF THE GREAT FEAST –
LUKE'S VERSION
Lk 14:15-24

14: 15 When one of those who sat at table with him heard this, he said to him, "Blessed is he who shall eat bread in the kingdom of God!" 16 But he said to him, "A man once gave a great banquet, and invited many; 17 and at the time for the banquet he sent his servant to say to those who had been invited, 'Come; for all is now ready.' But they all alike began to make excuses. The first said to him, 'I have bought a field, and I must go out and see it; I pray you, have me excused.' 19 And another said, 'I have bought five yoke of oxen, and I go to examine them; I pray you, have me excused.' 20 And another said, 'I have married a wife, and therefore I cannot come.' 21 So the servant came and reported this to his master. Then the householder in anger said to his servant, 'Go out quickly to the streets and lanes of the city, and bring in the poor and maimed and blind and lame.' 22 And the servant said, 'Sir, what you commanded has been done, and still there is room.' 23 And the master said to the servant, 'Go out to the highways and hedges, and compel people to come in, that my house may be filled. For I tell you, none of those men who were invited shall taste my banquet.' "

1.

Jesus' Conversation with His Contemporaries

The two accounts in Matthew and Luke are so similar to each other that they appear to be two versions of the same story. Especially noticeable is the similarity of plot: someone gives a banquet; the guests refuse to come; the host in anger orders that the people from the street be brought in; the purpose is to fill the banquet hall. And yet the two accounts are very different from each other, especially in the impact that they make. Matthew's version is full of vengeance taken by an angry king not only against the people who offended him, but also against their city. There follows the stern rejection of a poor soul who wandered in improperly dressed. Luke by contrast has a much more pleasing story of a host who seeks out the poor and unfortunate in a gracious gesture. Oddly enough, Luke's version ends with a stern note of rejection, as does Matthew's.

Several questions leap to the mind; Did Jesus tell such a story? If so, what was *his* version and for what purpose did he tell it? If the two versions go back to one story, who has changed one or the other and why? Many additional questions arise as we examine the passages closely.

We will claim that the story as Jesus told it is about people who exclude themselves from a great feast because they are busy with their own affairs. In this parable, Jesus warns his hearers that the kingdom of God is like a banquet which is *ready now*. If those who are invited do not come when called, they will not be included.

We will also claim that the parable has developed and changed. It is possible to trace something like a history of the parable. In doing so, one can enter into contact and conversation not only with Jesus but also with several different communities of the earliest church.

There are three steps which will help us to support these claims. These steps take us back in time from Matthew's and Luke's versions as we have them to the parable as Jesus originally told it.

THE FIRST STEP: A COMMON WRITTEN SOURCE

The first step in the reconstruction of the history of the parable is to see whether a common source can be discerned for the two versions we have. A preliminary exercise will aid in the search for a common source. We can look at the context in which the story appears in each Gospel. Are they the same? Did Matthew (Mt) and Luke (Lk) have a source in which this parable was part of a longer passage? The answer is negative. In Mt this parable follows another, the so-called Parable of the Vineyard (or of the Wicked Tenants, Mt 21:23-23:36). The Parable of the Great Feast in Mt is therefore part of a strong polemic between Jesus and his adversaries. His words are fighting words.

By contrast, Lk's version is found in a friendly setting. Jesus is at dinner with a Pharisee and others [Lk 14:1-24]. The talk at table is about dinners; our parable is the final unit in this section.

There is no indication, then, that either Mt or Lk has received the Parable of the Great Feast from a source which gives us the original context in which the parable was told. In attempting to reconstruct the possible source we must therefore rely on the two versions we have.

In seeking a possible common source, we look naturally at what is *common* to both versions and leave aside from consideration for the moment the differences between them. The common elements are:

a. The story begins with a reference to the kingdom of God/of heaven.
b. A man gave a great feast and sent his servant(s) to call the invited guests, saying, "Come, for all is now ready."

c. The guests refused to come. Either they made light of it and went off to their own affairs [Mt 22:5], or they made excuses that they had to attend to their own affairs [Lk 14:18-20].

d. The host in anger sent his servant(s) into the streets to invite as many as he (they) could find.

e. The purpose [Lk 14:23] or the result [Mt 22:10] of the host's action is to fill the banquet hall with guests.

f. The parable ends with the host's comment about the originally invited guests. Either [Lk 14:24] "For I tell you, none of those men who were invited shall taste my banquet," or [Mt 22:8] ". . . those invited were not worthy."

Both Mt 22:5 and Lk 14:18-20 expand on the refusal of the guests. This suggests that the source also did so. It is probable that Lk's three excuses belong to the source and that Mt has summarized them. There are traces in Mt of the three excuses in Lk:

a. One of Mt's invited guests "went off . . . to his *farm.*" This is similar to Lk's guest who has bought a *field.*

b. Mt has "oxen" on the menu. It may be that this is an echo of the excuse in Lk that someone has bought oxen.

c. In Mt, the great banquet has become a *marriage* feast. This may be an echo of Lk's third excuse, of the man who has recently *married.*

Each of these elements is a small one in itself, but together they strongly suggest that the three excuses of Lk, or something very similar to them, was in the source. It is much more likely that Mt has abbreviated the excuses than that Lk has picked up the "oxen" and "marriage" from the source and created three excuses from these small points.

Taking what is common to Mt and Lk (and including items from each which will need to be sorted out below), we can reconstruct the following coherent and complete parable:

The kingdom of God is like a man (a king) who gave a banquet (a marriage feast for his son) and sent his servant(s) to call the invited guests, saying, "Come, for

all is now ready." But they all alike began to make
excuses. The first said to him, "I have bought a field,
and I must go out and see it; I pray you, have me
excused." And another said, "I have bought five yoke of
oxen, and I go to examine them; I pray you, have me
excused." And another said, "I have married a wife, and
therefore I cannot come." So the servant(s) came and
reported this to his (their) master. Then the householder
was angry and said to his servant(s), "Go out into the
streets and invite as many as you find, and compel people
to come in, so that the banquet hall will be filled. For
none of those men who were invited shall taste of my
banquet."

We can make several observations about the parable as reconstructed. First, it is relatively easy to find a clear and coherent
story by using only those elements common to both Mt and Lk.
This fact strongly supports the thesis that there *was* such a source.
Second, where Mt and Lk disagree, but where the parable
requires one version or the other, we consider both and choose
between them. The parable as we have reconstructed it begins
with, "The kingdom of God may be compared. . . ." Here we
follow Mt rather than Lk for two reasons. The first is that so
many of the gospel parables begin this or a similar way, and it
seems to have been characteristic of parable beginnings. The
second reason is that we can see why Lk might have changed his
source. He wanted to connect the parable with the preceding
material as he had put it together. Jesus is in conversation with
other dinner guests. So Lk puts the reference to the kingdom
in the mouth of one of the other guests.
However, we follow Lk rather than Mt in choosing the phrase
"kingdom of God" over "kingdom of heaven" for our reconstruction of the source. We do this because "kingdom of heaven"
is a designation used only by Mt, never by Mark or Lk. (There
does not appear to be a difference in *meaning* in the two ways of
speaking about the kingdom.) It is reasonable to conclude, therefore, that Mt's source speaks of the "kingdom of God," and that

Mt has changed the phrase to "kingdom of heaven," as he has done so often in his gospel.

Third, when we reconstruct the source, its emphasis falls not on the guests who come in later, but on those who were invited first:

a. Their excuses are listed, an unnecessary element if the reader's attention is to be directed instead to the inviting of people off the streets.
b. Their reasons for refusing the invitation are all related to "business-as-usual." The banquet is not important enough to interrupt normal activities.
c. The host's anger at the original refusal is recorded.
d. The host's purpose in inviting others is not kindness or generosity, but to fill up the hall *so that* the originally invited guests will *not* get in.
e. The end, and therefore the climax, of the parable is the statement that the original set of guests will be excluded.

The story is then about people who exclude themselves from a great feast because they are busy with their own affairs. In this parable, Jesus warns his hearers that the kingdom of God is like a banquet which is *ready now*. If those who are invited do not come when called, they will not be included.

Was this story part of a longer source which contained material about Jesus' ministry? It appears so. There are many passages like this parable which appear in Mt and Lk but are not found elsewhere in the New Testament. That is, there are stories about Jesus which are so similar in Mt and Lk that these two gospel writers seem to have known the same source, yet they appear to have used it independently from each other. About one-fourth of Mt and one-fifth of Lk are composed of such material. When the accounts common to Mt and Lk are closely compared, they appear to form a collection of Jesus' teachings which students of the New Testament have called "Q" (which stands for *Quelle*, the German word for "source"). One of the major themes of this hypothetical source is Jesus' preaching about the coming kingdom. Q seems to have emerged in the Jewish-Christian church, probably no later than fifteen years after Jesus' death. It witnesses to the church's conviction that Jesus would soon return to inaugurate the kingdom of God on earth. Q was a collection of material about Jesus which early Jewish-Christians used in order to preach Jesus as the expected Messiah of and to the Jews, and to spread the message during whatever short period of time was left.

In such a setting, the Parable of the Great Feast, as we have reconstructed it, serves the church by proclaiming an urgent message: the kingdom is like a man whose banquet is ready *now*. If you who have awaited the Messiah and his kingdom for so long do not accept it now—if you go about your business as usual, as if nothing were happening—you may find that it is too late.

For Q, the "others" who will be invited in to the feast are not the Gentiles. There is no suggestion in Q of the mission to the Gentiles. The "others" were presumably those Jews who were not expected to qualify for entrance into the kingdom, like the tax collectors who collaborated with the hated Roman rulers, and others who were viewed as "outsiders" in the religious sense. But attention is not directed primarily to them in this parable. It is rather to the good and pious Jew, who hopes and awaits the Messiah and his kingdom, that the parable is addressed, as a warning.

There are some unanswered questions about the parable in Q as we have reconstructed it. Before going on to the next steps, it is useful to note them:

a. Was the host a "man" or a "king"?
b. Was the banquet a grand dinner party or a marriage feast for the king's son?
c. Was there one servant, or were there several sent out by the host?
d. How many times did someone go out after guests? In both Mt and Lk this takes place three times, but the reconstruction has only two. Why?
e. Where did the servant(s) go to find the "others"?
f. The reconstruction includes the host's words to the servant in Lk, "and compel people to come in." These words are not found in Mt. Why include them in Q?

g.   What light will be thrown on the parable by inquiry into the religion and culture of the time?

We will address the first five questions in taking the next step, and take up the last two questions in step three.

The first step, the search for a source common to Mt and Lk, has put us in touch with a Christian community which preserved and used the stories about Jesus some forty years before Mt and Lk wrote their gospels. Study of other passages common to Mt and Lk would teach us much more about this community. The modern reader, however, is already aware of the disparity between the Q community and twentieth century attitudes and concerns. We stand with this community in proclaiming Jesus as God's Messiah, but our diverse notions about the kingdom of God are very different from theirs; they thought that the time for making a decision to enter it was very short.

THE SECOND STEP: THE PARABLE AS IT WAS SPOKEN

The second step in the reconstruction of the history of the parable is to ask how the story was told *orally*. Before the stories about Jesus were written down, they were undoubtedly circulated by word of mouth. The settings were presumably diverse: the accounts could have been used in sermons, in instruction of new members of the community, in evangelism, in conversation. Various stories were perhaps told together, making little collections of traditions about Jesus. If we can get back to the oral form of the Parable of the Great Feast, we will be one step closer to its original telling by Jesus.

By attempting such a reconstruction, we are not moving in a simple chronological line. Stories continued to be *told* long after some people began writing them down. Indeed, the hypothetical source, Q, appears to stand very close to the oral tradition. That is, it does not seem to be a consciously *literary* composition, as do our gospels, Matthew, Mark, and Luke. However, changes occur between the telling and the writing down of stories, as the study of many ancient materials suggests. One important change which occurred either with Q or before the writing of Q was the shift in the language used. Jesus and his earliest followers presumably spoke Aramaic, the common language of their time and place. Q, as we can reconstruct it, was in Greek, the universal language of the Mediterranean world of the first century. The stories of Jesus' ministry can of course be translated from Greek back into Aramaic by specialists, and it is entirely possible that Q was originally written in Aramaic, but we have no documentary evidence of such a version.

Since much of Jesus' teaching available to us is in the form of parables, a great deal of study has been done on this kind of material, as well as on similar material, such as morality stories, folk tales, and historical sagas. The characteristics of the parable form evident in many parables can be distinguished. We can therefore compare our reconstruction of the version in Q with these typical features of the parable, and so reconstruct the way the story was originally told. The following points can be made with regard to the typical form of the parable and the reconstruction of the Parable of the Great Feast.

First, a parable is either a metaphor or simile. Something is said to be "like" something else. In the Parable of the Great Feast, the kingdom of God is *like*—not a *man* or *king*, but *like the whole story*: host, invitation, refusals, anger, another invitation, other guests, purpose, final statement. The story-teller illustrates his crucial term, the kingdom, by analogy to a familiar event, a dinner party. The kingdom is not explained or described in literal terms; it is *pictured* by comparing it to a known human event.

All of the elements in a parable contribute to the overall impact of the story. This is usually said in a different way, namely, that a parable has only one point. But this is too limited a way of looking at the material; nuances important to the total experience of the parable can be lost. What is intended in either statement is to distinguish the parable from its cousin, the allegory. In allegories each individual element in an account stands for, represents, something else; it has a symbolic meaning, as in the most famous allegory known to English readers, Bunyan's *Pilgrim's Progress*. The distinction between parable and allegory is important for discussing our parable. The host does not, in the reconstruction, represent God. It is not said that God is angry, or that God "compels" people to come into the kingdom of God. On the contrary, there are no elements in the reconstruction which require an allegorical interpretation.

Second, it is characteristic of the parable that it moves forward with a great economy of plot and words. Many questions are left unanswered; only those characters and actions necessary to the teller's intention, in his own context, are included. In the case of the Parable of the Great Feast, the reconstruction makes clear that the dominant message is: Come now to the feast (the kingdom) or you will discover that you have excluded yourselves. But the parable contains more than just the "message."

For the moment, however, we are in a position to address some of the questions listed above. The host was surely a neutral "man" and not a "king"; the feast was just that, not a marriage banquet. The king and marriage feast for the son are elements in the story which *divert* the attention from the central thrust of the parable. (They are also, of course, in the early church, allegorical features: the "king" is God; the "son" is the Son of God, Jesus Christ; the marriage feast is an image to represent the joy of the coming kingdom.) There was one servant sent, not several. The story only needs one. The introduction of several is again distracting. The listener/reader asks: whom do these represent? Attention is focused on the servants, where it patently does not belong.

In the Q source, one servant was sent out twice, once to call the originally invited guests and then once more to call in the "others." We will need to ask below why Mt has sent servants twice to the originally invited guests, and why Lk has sent a servant twice into the streets and lanes to get others to fill the hall. For the moment, we notice that one set of people rejected the invitation and one set was brought into the banquet unexpectedly. These two sets of people only require two errands on the part of the servant.

The servant in the reconstructed source went to the *streets* looking for people to bring into the banquet hall. In Mt, the host sends the servants to the "thoroughfares" (vs 9); the servants went out into the "streets" (vs 10). In Lk, the servant was sent first "to the streets and lanes of the city" (vs 21), then to the "highways and hedges" (vs 23). The simple term, "streets" appears in both versions. It is probable that each gospel author has expanded the source.

Third, it is characteristic of the oral parable that it often moves forward by a series-of-three motif. It is partly for this reason that our Q version includes the three excuses of those who refused to come to the dinner. It is the way so many stories of all kinds are *told*. One has only to think of all the jokes about three ministers who die and go to heaven.

Finally, it appears to be typical of Jesus' parables that they end with a sharp challenge, that they are open-ended in such a way as to invite or perhaps demand responses of the listeners. It is in part for this reason that our reconstruction ends as it does.

In tracing the history of the development of the parable back from the versions in Mt and Lk, we have now moved *two* steps. The first was to uncover the parable as Mt and Lk received it in their source, Q. The second was to test that source to see if it conformed to the way in which the parable might have been told orally, before it was written down and became part of a collection of stories about Jesus. Since our parable is so like the typical way in which parables were told, we conclude that Q has incorporated the parable as it was circulated in the oral story-telling period.

THE THIRD STEP: HOW DID JESUS TELL HIS PARABLE?

The third step in the reconstruction of the history of the parable is to try to determine whether Jesus told it, and, if he did, what he intended by it and how it was understood by his listeners.

It is important to note that these stories were remembered and circulated by people whose lives had been gripped and overturned by an extraordinary series of events. The leader in whom they had placed their hopes had been crucified, the one who had brought hope to his people had been rejected and destroyed. Suddenly they knew that in spite of this death, or more accurately, beyond it, Jesus was alive; God had raised him from the dead. The Holy Spirit was poured out on these people, and they knew the crucified and risen Jesus as the Messiah long promised to Israel. They set about to proclaim this amazing message. It would be very surprising, to say the least, if this radical reversal of affairs had made no impact at all on their memories of Jesus' ministry among them. It would be equally astonishing if they did not use their memories of Jesus to proclaim him as Messiah.

If genuine conversation with Jesus as well as with the various voices from the earliest church is our objective, it is useful to distinguish the various voices as carefully as we can. A series of tests can be applied to the stories about Jesus which help to identify what he said and did, in contrast to later memories of him. We will apply these tests to the Parable of the Great Feast.

First, does a given report, saying, or parable appear in more than one ancient source known to us? We ask this question because there is much evidence to suggest that some of the earliest churches developed along relatively independent lines. Q does not mention a Christian mission to the Gentiles, but such a mission had surely begun before Q was written. Paul's letters give little evidence that he knew the stories about Jesus' ministry. There are only a few stories about Jesus which are common to the first three gospels (Mt, Mk, Lk) on the one hand, and John, on the other. If, then, a story is found in two or more of these relatively independent writings, it probably comes from a very early time, before the communities which produced them began to go their separate ways. Positive results from this test do not *prove* that we are in touch with Jesus, but they put us very close to him.

Is the Parable of the Great Feast found in more than one ancient source? Mt and Lk do not count as *two* sources, since both appear to be dependent upon a prior source, Q. A second possible source is the Gospel of Thomas, a collection of Jesus' teachings which was written long after our gospels. It appears, however, to contain much very early material. It also appears to be independent of our gospel sources. The relevant passage from the Gospel of Thomas is as follows:

Thomas 64. Jesus said: A man had guest-friends, and when he had prepared the dinner, he sent his servant to invite the guest-friends. He went to the first, he said to him: "My master invites thee." He said: "I have some claims against some merchants; they will come to me in the evening; I will go and give them my orders. I pray to be excused from the dinner." He went to another, he said to him: "My master has invited thee." He said to him: "I have bought a house and they request me for a day. I will have no time." He came to another, he said to him: "My master invites thee." He said to him: "My friend is to be married and I am to arrange a dinner; I shall not be able to come. I pray to be excused from the dinner." He went to another, he said to him: "My master invites thee." He said to him: "I have bought a farm, I go to collect the rent. I shall not be able to come. I pray to be excused." The servant came, he said to his master: "Those whom thou hast invited to the dinner have excused themselves." The master said to his servant: "Go out to the roads, bring those whom thou shalt find, so that they may dine. Tradesmen and merchants [shall] not [enter] the places of my Father."

Several elements in this version appear to be additions typical of the community in which the Gospel of Thomas was produced: the shift from a rural to an urban environment, the bias against "buyers and merchants," the addition of a fourth excuse. Allowing for such changes, the underlying source looks very like our reconstruction of the parable at the stage of its circulation orally. We conclude therefore that we probably have a second, independent source for the Parable of the Great Feast in the Gospel of Thomas. We know of no other sources.

A second test which will help to identify what Jesus actually said, in contrast to later memories of his words, is a historical one: are the conditions presupposed in the parable (economic, social, cultural, religious, political, linguistic) those of Jesus' own time and situation, as compared with conditions characteristic of the later churches? An affirmative answer to this question, like the question about multiple sources, will not *prove* that Jesus told his parable in these words, but it will help to distinguish possible additions to his version.

There are several important points to note:

a. A rural setting, characteristic of Galilee in Jesus' time, is suggested by the first two excuses. One man has bought a field, another five yoke of oxen. The latter item tells us that the social circle of the invited guests is an affluent one. Not many Galilean farmers could afford so many oxen, nor had so much land to work as to need so many.

b. We understand the third excuse, that one of the guests had married a wife and therefore could not come, when we note that in Jesus' time, women were not invited to such banquets. In addition, Deuteronomy 24:5 tells us that a newly-married man is exempt from various duties. It is possible that this text was interpreted in Jesus' day to include social obligations.

c. The customs of courtesy in Jesus' time help to illumine the parable. For example, it was customary when giving a large and important party, to issue *two* invitations. The first alerted the invited guests to the day; the second was a call to come when the feast was ready. The double invitation was a special mark of courtesy. One ancient Jewish source comments, "None of them [the invited] would attend a banquet unless he was invited twice." The parable clearly presupposes this custom. If the modern reader is sympathetic to the guest who is apparently supposed to drop everything and to respond to a last-minute invitation or be excluded, it helps to know that the originally invited guests have known all along that this second summons was coming.

d. Another ancient courtesy sheds light on the odd command of the host to "compel people to come in." It was customary for the guests to hang back when called to a dinner. The host or servant then urged, insisted, compelled the guests in. Such urging would be all the more necessary for people suddenly called in off the streets. It is also a striking note in the parable that such people are treated with great courtesy, and not as if they were the recipients of benevolent charity. The word "compel" belongs, then, to the parabolic picture. It is not a description, for example, of God compelling people to come into the Kingdom of God.

e. We move closer to the heart of the parable if we ask what sort of imagery was used to describe the kingdom by Jews in Jesus' time. Was the feast a common metaphor employed? The answer is an emphatic yes. Lk's introduction to this parable suggests such a link: "Blessed is he who shall eat bread in the kingdom of God!" There is a saying also from Q: "And they will come from east and west and from north and south, and sit at table in the kingdom of God" [Lk 13:29; see also Mt 8:11]. In Rev 19:9 we read, "And the angel said to me, 'Write this: Blessed are those who are invited to the marriage supper of the Lamb.' " But we must get behind the Christian materials if we are to document the imagery in *Jesus'* time. There are a number of texts in the Old Testament, which was Scripture for Jesus and his contemporaries, which can be cited:

> "On this mountain the Lord of hosts will make for all peoples a feast of fat things, of wine. . . ." [Isaiah 25:6].

> "I will feast the soul of the priests with abundance, and my people will be satisfied with my goodness, says the Lord" [Jeremiah 31:14].

These and other texts from the Old Testament are found in passages where the coming victory of the Lord is under discussion. God's final salvation is described in the imagery of feasting. The same is true of many Jewish sources closer to Jesus's time. The following examples are typical:

Ethiopic Enoch 62:14: "The Lord of Spirits will dwell over them, and they will eat and lie down and rise up to all eternity with that Son of Man."

Slavonic Enoch 42:5: "At the last coming he will lead out Adam and the patriarchs and bring them [into the paradise of Eden] that they may rejoice, as when a man invites his friends to eat with him, and they come and speak with one another before the palace, joyously awaiting his feast, the enjoyment of good things, of immeasurable wealth and joy and happiness in light and everlasting life."

II Esdras (IV Ezra) 2:38: "Rise and stand, and see at the feast of the Lord the number of those who have been sealed."

Midrash Esther 1:14: "The feast of our God, which he will prepare for the righteous, has no end."

Many other examples could be given. The basic metaphor— the kingdom is like a feast—was widely known and used in Jewish circles.

For Jesus to tell a parable in which the kingdom of God is likened to a great feast is therefore a strong argument for the claim that the parable indeed goes back to Jesus. His listeners are completely with him at the beginning of the parable, comfortable with the well-known metaphor he is using.

A third test that will help to identify what Jesus actually said, in contrast to later memories of his words, is the test of *distinctiveness.* This is the most stringent test of the four and yields the most reliable information, from a historian's perspective. We ask: are Jesus' words distinct *both* from the Judaism of his time *and* from the interests of the later church? Of course, much of Jesus' teaching had a lot in common with his own time and people. We have just noted that he used a common Jewish image for the kingdom, namely, the feast. It is also, of course, true that the earliest church *followed* Jesus and was consistent with his teaching. The early Christians were the ones who saved the stories which make up the gospels. If we were to accept as truly Jesus' words only those which are distinct from his own setting and his own followers, we would rule out a lot of what he undoubtedly taught.

Nevertheless, where we can identify teaching which is clearly unique to Jesus, we are obviously on very reliable ground as we seek to hear his own voice speaking. At two crucial points in the Parable of the Great Feast, teaching unique to Jesus is clearly apparent. The first is the statement, "Come, for all is now ready." In Jesus' setting, that is a very radical claim indeed. Many Jews of his day longed for the coming of the kingdom feast; some believed that it would surely come soon. But the announcement that the kingdom feast was ready *now* would have startled Jesus' hearers considerably. Where were the expected signs? Why did the skies not open? Where was the triumph of God, visible for all to see? The kingdom banquet was *now* spread out? Drop everything and come? Why? Why would anyone believe such a drastic and unlikely announcement? As the parable unfolds, it is clear that most people would not believe it. On the contrary, they believed that there was still time for business-as-usual.

The claim, "Come, for all is now ready," is also distinct from the message of the church as it was proclaimed by the time of Mt and Lk. In the earlier period, discussed above, Christians used the parable by way of proclaiming their urgent message: come now before it is too late. But by the time of Mt and Lk, as we shall see below, the expected kingdom had not, in fact, come, and each gospel author changed the parable in order to deal with the situation of his own church.

The second place in the Parable of the Great Feast where we find teaching unique to Jesus is in the calling of those who come into the banquet hall. Who were the long-ago invited guests, those with a right to expect invitations to the kingdom feast? Surely they were those Jews who received and transmitted the promise of God's kingdom, those who longed and hoped for it, those who where loyal to the conditions for entry into it. There is an old Jewish saying:

If all the Jews in all the world would keep the Law totally
and completely for 24 hours, the kingdom would come.

There is nothing self-righteous or picayune about that aphorism.
It speaks of longing for the kingdom and also of the heavy respon-
sibility laid on faithful Jews. It is both wistful and wise.

The impact made by this parable on Jesus' listeners would
have been shocking. For the parable does *not* say that those who
should get in actually join the feast; those who have always known
that places at the kingdom table were reserved for them do not in
fact get in. Unidentified "others" are the ones to enter the
banquet hall. The parable would surely have astonished both sets
of people.

A very old Jewish story, perhaps known to Jesus and his
listeners, will illustrate the point:

> Two pious men lived together in Ashkelon, devoting them-
> selves to the study of the Law. One of them died and no
> honor was paid to him at his funeral. Bar Ma'yon, a tax
> collector, died and the whole town honored his funeral.
> The remaining pious man was deeply disturbed and cried
> out that the wicked in Israel did not get their deserts.
> But his dead companion appeared to him in a dream and
> told him not to despise the ways of God in Israel. He
> himself had committed one evil deed and hence had suf-
> fered dishonor at his funeral, whereas Bar Ma'yon had
> committed one good deed and for that had been honored
> at his. What evil deed had the pious man committed?
> On one occasion he had put on his phylacteries in the
> wrong order. What good deed had the tax collector com-
> mitted? Once he had given a breakfast for the leading men
> of the town and they had not come. So he gave orders
> that the poor were to be invited to eat it, that it should not
> go to waste. After some days the pious man saw his dead
> companion walking in the garden of paradise beside
> fountains of water; and he saw Bar Ma'yon the tax

collector lying on the bank of a river; he was striving to reach the water and he could not.*

In both this story and the parable there is a banquet given to which the originally invited guests refuse to come, and others are brought in. There the resemblance ends. The Jewish story illustrates the notion of exact reward for good and evil deeds; the parable completely upsets the notion of exact reward and punishment. That would be surprising enough. When the "reward" is the *kingdom* banquet, the upsetting of normal notions is drastic indeed.

Is this point about the wrong people getting into the kingdom banquet also distinct from the earliest Christians' message? Of course it is not. The parable after all was preserved by the earliest Christians. It is to be noted, however, that Mt, whose version we will consider in the next chapter, saw fit at least to qualify the original message by adding the short parable of the man incorrectly dressed (a common metaphor for behavior) who was allowed in and then expelled. The church since Mt's time has not always taken with great seriousness this word about who finally are the right and wrong people.

The fourth test which will help to identify what Jesus actually said, in contrast to later memories of his words, is a question of *coherence*. We ask: is the parable consistent with the most reliable information we have about Jesus? Once again, the answer is decidedly in the affirmative. Not only is it everywhere reported that Jesus frequently associated with outcasts, sinners, tax collectors and the like. It is also a marked feature of many of these stories that he ate with them. There is a report of such a meal in Mk 2:15-17, with parallel accounts in both Mt and Lk. One thinks of Zacchaeus in Lk 19:1-10, into whose house Jesus invited

---

*The story is found in the Palestinian Talmud, *j.* Shanh. 6.23c. Our version is a free translation from original Aramaic by Norman Perrin in *Rediscovering the Teachings of Jesus*, pp. 111f.

himself. Other examples abound. There is more at stake in these
meals than kindness to the poor or carelessness about the laws of
purity. In a setting where the feast is such a common metaphor
for the kingdom, when the one who comes preaching the kingdom
sits down with others to eat, he is in fact *acting out the presence
of the kingdom banquet*. By his actions, Jesus said the same thing
our parable says: the kingdom banquet is now being celebrated.
And just look at who gets to come!

Each of these tests to help identify what Jesus actually said
indicates separately that the parable as we have reconstructed it
is the one he told his listeners. Together, the four tests offer
strong evidence for this conclusion.

Jesus' conversations with his contemporaries took place, like
all human encounters, at specific times and places, and under
specific circumstances. We do not know what these were in any
detail. We do not know who heard him tell the Parable of the
Great Feast. It is well then not to limit this audience by assum-
ing, for example, that he addressed only his opponents or his
friends. Like other wandering teachers of his time, he probably
addressed a motley group composed of various sorts of people.
Some were surely his friends and followers, disciples who accom-
panied him. Others may have included the merely curious, those
who will always come out to hear a teacher. There were probably
some who were intrigued by Jesus, but who had not made up
their minds about him. There were surely some poor unfortunates, like the beggars and physically handicapped, who gathered in
public places. And there were probably those who were uneasy
about him, who saw him as a potential trouble-maker, who
watched him, checked up on what he did and said. It is a mistake
to think of these latter, the Jewish establishment of the day, as
self-righteous, hypocritical straw men Christians often set up in
their minds when they think of Pharisees and scribes. Some of
these did indeed clash with Jesus, but the battle was not about
petty legalism or contemptuous treatment of the poor and outcasts—their record on this score was among the best in the ancient
world. Exactly *what* the conflict was between Jesus and his
opponents is an issue to be inquired into.

Jesus invited, demanded, a response. The Parable of the Great Feast is told in a way that requires a response. One could walk away, but one could not very well remain and be neutral. The parable is part of an ongoing confrontation. When the parable ended, we may be sure that the discussion did not.

How would Jesus' listeners have heard and responded to the Parable of the Great Feast? They would surely have been with him at the beginning. Here is something they know about: the coming, expected, hoped-for kingdom, like a banquet. People will gather around a table to rejoice and celebrate. (Unlike the Jewish story cited above, about two men who die and go to their respective rewards, this parable is about a *people* who gather, *not* about individual destiny.) So there are no surprises at the beginning of the parable. Those who knew Jesus or something about him knew that he seemed always to be teaching about the kingdom of God.

It is possible that the statement, "Come, for all is now ready," might have occasioned some surprise among the more alert of Jesus' listeners, but early in the parable, perhaps not. The meaning of "all is now ready" will depend on how the story proceeds. It would become clear, however, that Jesus was not talking about some far-off event, but rather an imminent one. Some of his listeners surely believed that the kingdom would soon come.

The first really striking and surprising element in the parable would have been the refusal of *all* the invited guests. Of course, this is a story—in real life, one or two might have to cancel at the last minute, but not everyone would do so. This parable about a familiar event—a dinner party—is going to have some peculiar twists. If Jesus' listeners knew the story quoted above about the two men who died and got their respective rewards, they would have been alert to hear how Jesus would tell a similar story.

The three excuses would have brought chuckles from Jesus' audience. The listeners would appreciate the comedy. The excuses build toward a comic climax. A man has bought a field and *after* paying for it, goes to see it? At sundown, dinnertime? Peculiar, to say the least. Similarly (to drive home the comic point?), another has bought five yoke of oxen—and only now, after paying and as the light begins to fade, he goes to examine them? What kind of excuses are these? The third excuse is the last straw. Another guest has been married. How was it that he accepted the invitation to the banquet in the first place, if his wedding had already been planned? And why had the host not known of the marriage; why was he not invited to the wedding? Jesus' listeners would have appreciated the fact that the excuses were *parodies* of business-as-usual. Reasonable business and personal motives for missing a banquet are exposed as trivial and thoughtless when they are made into last-minute excuses. Of those who made the excuses, one friend of mine said, "You just know that you can't believe a word they say!"

The host's anger was plainly justified. He had been badly snubbed. What will he do to save his banquet? Like the tax collector in the story, who was also snubbed by the town's important men, the host sent a servant to round up anyone he could find in the streets and bring them in.

Listeners' responses would have been diverse. Some of the poor, not likely ever to be invited to such a grand affair, may have felt a wry satisfaction that a rich host for once got his comeuppance. For some, the reaction may have been embarrassment at the lengths to which the host went to save his ruined party. Some were surely offended that someone who could afford such a grand dinner would do such a thing. (Think of the damage to the house, the possibility of theft!) Some of the less fortunate might have imagined that, had the story been real, they would have had a chance to get in.

If some of the listeners had heard the Jewish story cited above, they would have noted the curious twist that Jesus gave it: the purpose in the two stories is the same, to avoid wasting the food, to fill the banquet hall. But Jesus' parable is about the *kingdom* banquet. This parable is not about an isolated kindness to the less fortunate; it is about those who will be included at God's table.

And imagine the people who were brought in! We usually think of them as the poor and crippled, because Lk describes them as such. But Jesus did not specify these. The servant is told to bring anyone and everyone he found. Who were these likely to be, gathered in the village square at sundown? A very mixed group surely: the beggars who were always there, of course, but also shop-keepers closing up for the day, farmers gathered to talk a little before going home to dinner, even some Pharisees and scribes. The group suggested by Jesus included the respectable and the disreputable, the well-off and the poor, the clean and the dirty. The thought of this unlikely group all crowding into the banquet hall together must have made Jesus' listeners laugh.

The real shocker in the parable is that the purpose of bringing the "others" in is to fill the banquet hall. The consequence is that those who first refused the invitation will not get in at all. At the end of the parable it becomes clear that the call, "Come, for all is now ready," and the excuses due to business-as-usual, constitute something very like *judgment*. We noted above that the parable as a whole has a strong focus on the originally invited guests. There is another note also: those who never expected an invitation are included. This note is not to be missed, and certainly Jesus' original listeners did not miss it. But the dominant note is that those who do not come when called will not get in at all. The reverse, of course, is also true. Those who come when called *will* get in, all of them.

The offense for the good (and they really were good, better than most of us), law-abiding Jewish listeners was double. First, this wandering teacher without any credentials tells them that the hour is *now*; there will soon be a time when it will be *too late*. He makes fun of their seriousness about normal, business-as-usual living; he shows it up as trivial when confronted with the kingdom invitation. The second offense is that anyone, just anyone who will come, will be included.

For those among his listeners who knew something of Jesus, the link between the parable and Jesus' carelessness about dinner companions would be clear. He ate with both the Pharisees and tax collectors. The urgent question raised is: what sort of kingdom is being pictured? The parable challenges sharply the normal assumptions about the kingdom and the qualifications for entering it, both for those who thought they would be included and for those who thought they did not have a chance to get in.

For modern listeners to the Parable of the Great Feast, there are some questions to ponder. If Jesus said that the kingdom banquet is ready *now*, what does that mean to people who listen to him almost two thousand years later? In what sense did Jesus inaugurate the kingdom? The world as we experience it does not conform to any image we can think of for the kingdom of God. We are instructed by the fact that for Jesus, the kingdom was not an individual experience, as we so often think of it. If not that, then what? What, for example, does it mean to respond to the call, "Come, for all is now ready"? What does that call promise us? To what does it call us?

2.

Matthew and Luke Join the Conversation

Our first reaction to Mt's and Lk's versions of the Parable of the
Great Feast, when we compare it to the reconstruction of Q,
ranges anywhere from puzzlement to outrage. Mt and Lk have
changed the parable Jesus told. The first question we ask is not
"Why?", but "How dare they?" Who did they think they were to
change the words of Jesus? The analysis of the last chapter
suggests that Jesus' parable was preserved in the oral story-telling
of the earliest church and in the Q version. Q, as we can reconstruct it, was in Greek, not in the Aramaic Jesus spoke. But apart
from the translation Q seems to have been faithful to the story,
unlike Mt and Lk. What possessed Mt and Lk to make them think
they had the freedom to revise? It is something we would never
do intentionally. We want Jesus' words. Do we have them in the
gospels? Or do we have instead an unreliable hodge-podge of
Jesus' teaching along with that of a lot of nameless first-century
Christians? Do we lose Jesus the teacher in return for the teaching of the earliest followers of Jesus?

Several points offer a preliminary answer to these questions.
First of all, Mt and Lk were not the first to make changes in the
stories about Jesus. Analysis of other passages suggests that such
changes go back in some cases to the very earliest retelling of the
stories. Second, Mt and Lk were not trying to obliterate the
stories they received. If Mt and Lk knew the source Q, their
readers surely also knew it. They were therefore aware that Mt
and Lk were making changes in the parable. Third, it is important
to note that Mt and Lk have both allowed anomalies to remain in
their versions, which we will look at in a moment. To take the
most obvious example: in his version, Mt has an unfortunate soul
dragged in off the streets to the feast and then thrown into "outer

darkness" because he is not properly dressed. Why should he be punished for what was not his fault? Oddities such as this are found in both versions. Mt and Lk could easily have smoothed them out, but they did not. It is as if they are inviting their readers (including us) to do a little work on their stories.

However, we are still facing uncertainty even after these points have been made. Why would Mt and Lk change the parable? There are several clues which point toward an answer. One clue is that Jesus *told* the parable; Mt and Lk are writing gospels. Telling is different from writing and hearing is different from reading. For one thing, the writer knows that his readers can see the story in its context; for another, he knows that his readers can go back and reread what is written.

A second clue is offered by the fact that Mt and Lk wrote *gospels*. Why write a gospel? If you have something to say, why not just say it? Paul, whose letters are our earliest Christian writings, did just that. Why did Mt and Lk choose the gospel as the vehicle for their messages, if they were not intending to record the events accurately? As we will see, the Parable of the Great Banquet is a somewhat awkward means for putting forward the message of each author. Why use it, then?

Mt and Lk used the gospel as the vehicle to address their contemporaries because they were participating in a double conversation. On the one hand, they were in conversation with Jesus. We have seen that Jesus invited, perhaps even demanded, response to his teaching. This parable and others were told by him in order to get people involved as participants. It was the genius of Jesus' teaching, and especially of his parables, that they disallowed passive reception; they required active response. We do not have any written record of how Jesus' original hearers reacted to his telling of this parable, but we know how Mt and Lk reacted. They accepted Jesus' invitation, his challenge; they joined the conversation. Their rewriting of the stories Jesus told is their response to his invitation. The story of Jesus had great authority for them—it was THE STORY. So they told it.

On the other hand, Mt and Lk were in conversation with their own contemporaries, who lived roughly at the end of the first century of the Christian era (C. E.). Like other New Testament authors, Mt and Lk took seriously their received tradition—the Old Testament, the literature and belief of their own time, the church's claims about Jesus Christ. Unlike all other New Testament writers except Mark and John, they used the gospel as the vehicle for their message. Since their own situations called for response and action, they *changed* the stories they received about Jesus in order to allow them to address new situations. They asked their readers: does it help us to tell the stories *this way*?

For Mt and Lk, the stories were "sacred" not in the sense that they could not be tampered with, but in the sense that they were a powerful means of calling the Christians of their own day to obedience and mission. Both gospel writers had enormous respect for the material they used. They also had great freedom in how they used it.

A third clue about why Mt and Lk changed the stories of Jesus is the fact that their gospels (like Mark and John) were written anonymously. We are interested in who wrote the gospels, as Christians have been from the beginning, so that names and geographical and historical settings have been attached to each gospel. Whether they are true or not is impossible to know. But it is interesting and instructive to note that the gospel authors did not sign their works. Why not? One possible reason is that they understood themselves to be speaking in their own communities and not simply to them. They stood with their readers, not over against them as authorities. They are authoritative for us in a way that they were not for their contemporaries. They asked their readers: does it help *us* to tell the story this way?

To listen in on their conversations with Jesus and with their own fellow Christians is to be invited to join the conversation ourselves.

Q

The kingdom of God is like a man who gave a banquet and sent his servant to call the invited guests, saying, "Come, for all is now ready." But they all alike began to make excuses. The first said to him, "I have bought a field, and I must go and see it; I pray you, have me excused." And another said, "I have bought five yoke of oxen, and I go to examine them; I pray you, have me excused." And another said, "I have married a wife, and therefore I cannot come." So the servant came and reported this to his master. Then the householder was angry and said to his servant, "Go out into the streets and invite as many as you find, and compel people to come in, so that the banquet hall will be filled. For none of those men who were invited shall taste of my banquet.

THE PARABLE OF THE GREAT FEAST –
MATTHEW'S VERSION
Mt 22:1-14

22: 1 And again Jesus spoke to them in parables, saying,
2 "The kingdom of heaven may be compared to a king who gave a marriage feast for his son, 3 and sent his servants to call those who were invited to the marriage feast, but they would not come. 4 Again he sent other servants, saying, 'Tell those who are invited, Behold I have made ready my dinner, my oxen and my fat calves are killed, and everything is ready; come to the marriage feast.' 5 But they made light of it and went off, one to his farm, another to his business, 6 while the rest seized his servants, treated them shamefully, and killed them. 7 The king was angry, and he sent his troops and destroyed those murderers and burned their city. 8Then he said to his servants, 'The wedding is ready, but those invited were not worthy. 9 Go therefore to the thoroughfares, and invite to the marriage feast as many as you find.' 10 And those servants went out into the streets and gathered all whom they found, both bad and good; so the wedding hall was filled with guests.

11 But when the king came in to look at the guests, he saw there a man who had no wedding garment; 12 and he said to him, 'Friend, how did you get in here without a wedding garment?' And he was speechless. 13 Then the king said to the attendants, 'Bind him hand and foot, and cast him into the outer darkness; there men will weep and gnash their teeth.' 14 For many are called, but few are chosen."

How has Mt changed the parable, and why? Mt has altered the parable's impact in three ways. First, he has changed elements in the parable itself. Second, he has added to it a further story, the little Parable of the Wedding Garment. Third, he has set both in their present context in his Gospel. What do these changes tell us about Mt's interpretation of the parable? We will look at the three things he has done.

First, Mt has made the following alterations in the parable itself:

a. The host has become a king.
b. The dinner party has become a marriage feast for his son.
c. One servant has become two sets of servants.
d. The first sending of the servants to call the guests is reported briefly and undramatically.
e. The second group of servants is sent by the host, who says twice that "everything is ready" and names the dishes, indicating that the feast is a very grand one indeed.
f. The reaction of the invited guests is expanded: some react as in the Q version of the parable although their excuses are not quoted; others seize, mistreat, and kill the servants.
g. The king's anger is vented on the murderers. He sends his army to kill them and destroy their city.
h. The king then repeats the statement that the banquet is ready and adds that the originally invited guests were not "worthy."
i. Those brought in off the streets are both "good and bad."
j. The wedding hall is filled with guests.

What is striking about the parable in Mt is its ferocity. Some of the invited guests kill some of the servants, and in return the king sends his troops to kill them and to destroy their city. These actions are very strange in the context of the parable. The feast which is ready awaits the guests while a war is fought. It is clear that Mt has transformed the parable into an allegory. What would his readers have thought when they read about the destruction of the city? It is not difficult to answer this question. In 70 C.E., Roman armies brought to a climax their four year war in Judea by destroying Jerusalem. This event was a devastating blow to Jews and to Jewish Christians, and Mt clearly refers to it in his reworking of the Parable of the Great Feast.

Other allegorical features are equally obvious. The king, in this kingdom parable, is God. The son is Jesus Christ, the Son of God. The feast as an image of the kingdom has become the marriage feast of the son. Would Mt's readers be familiar with this last image? It does not seem that a *marriage* dinner was an image for the kingdom in Judaism, but it clearly functioned that way in the earliest church. The New Testament offers a number of texts in which the church is described as the bride of Christ (such as Eph 5:21-33 and Rev 21:9). Closer to the traditions about Jesus is the account in Mk 2:19-20, where Jesus refers to himself as the bridegroom and to his feasting as the marriage banquet. Mt's readers probably knew Mark's gospel, just as they knew Q. This story also appears in Mt 9:14-17. In our parable, then, the marriage feast certainly suggests the kingdom of God as preached by Christian evangelists, and the church as the witness to the kingdom.

The two sets of servants sent to call the invited guests are allegorical figures representing those who witness to the kingdom. The first set, to which little attention is given, may represent the prophets of Israel who long ago prophesied the kingdom. The second set, some of whom were mistreated and murdered, are surely the Christian evangelists of Mt's church. Who were the invited guests? Surely the Jews, who had long hoped for and awaited the coming of the kingdom. In Mt's version of the parable, the Jews not only refuse to come but also treat the messengers with violence. The readers would not miss the point: Christian witnesses to the kingdom suffer violence at the hands of those to whom the kingdom has been promised. It is also possible that they along with Mt, know of some actual cases where violence has been done to Christian evangelists.

Mt interprets the Roman destruction of Jerusalem, the capital of Judaism, as God's punishment of the Jews for refusing to respond to the Christian message. He did not invent this idea, for it is found in all four gospels (Mt 24:1-2; Mk 13:1-2; Lk 21:6; Jn 2:19). So this notion was abroad in some churches prior to Mt's work, but Mt has developed it and made it unmistakeably clear in his version of this parable.

We note that the fact that the marriage feast is "ready" is repeated three times in Mt's version of the parable, compared to only once in the reconstructed Q version. In this connection the wedding hall is *filled* with guests, whereas in the Q parable the host's *intention* is to fill the hall. We are drawn to ask if Mt wants to equate the kingdom to the church, to those who are already in the church. But this cannot be his intention, since elsewhere in his gospel Mt both expresses the hope for the *coming* of the kingdom and records Jesus' sending his disciples out to mission. Why, then, the heavy emphasis on the readiness of the banquet *now* and on the hall which is already filled? Perhaps Mt sees that the division between those who will enter the kingdom and those who will not has begun in his own time. Thus he stresses the urgency of the choice. He also excludes as "unworthy" those invited who refused to come and who mistreat the messengers. A very stern judgment indeed.

These are the alterations Mt has made in the body of the parable. To go on with our investigation, we look at the end of the parable, where Mt changes its impact by adding the little Parable of the Wedding Garment. This addition provides one answer to our question of why the hall is filled. Mt has the hall filled so that he can go on to talk about those who got in. There is a shift in attention away from those who excluded themselves and got destroyed for it, to those who have been brought in. These, he tells us in the parable, were "both good and bad." The appended Parable of the Wedding Garment explains why Mt has used these words to describe those brought in off the streets.

The Parable of the Wedding Garment was clearly not originally part of the Parable of the Great Feast. Not only does Lk have no hint of it, it also does not fit the present location. Why would someone dragged in off the street at a moment's notice be thrown out because he is not correctly dressed? Mt has added this parable, which may have circulated independently at first, without bothering to smooth out the difficulty. He expects his readers to move along with him in the allegory he is presenting.

The Parable of the Wedding Garment is cryptic, to say the least. As in so many parables, questions arise: why does the guest not answer? Why is he cast into "outer darkness" instead of just "out"? What does the final comment, "Many are called, but few are chosen," mean?

It is well not to jump too quickly to a neat interpretation of the parable. One imagines that Mt's readers paused for thought and perhaps they discussed it among themselves. However, one or two comments are in order. The wedding garment is surely an allegorical symbol, as are so many other elements in the passage, and at least two meanings lie close at hand. One is the use of the term "garment" to represent repentance, a metaphor found in Jewish literature of Mt's time. Another is the symbol of the garment as righteousness. In Isaiah 61:10, for example, we read:

For [God] has clothed me with the garments of salvation,
he has covered me with the robe of righteousness,
as a bridegroom decks himself with a garland,
and as a bride adorns herself with her jewels.

The proper "garment" for those who come to the kingdom feast is that of God's salvation, God's giving of righteousness. Mt seems to be saying that while the invitation to anyone and everyone is open, and those who come in are both "good and bad," one's presence at the banquet is not thereby guaranteed. Many may be called, but only those who respond in terms of God's invitation— with repentance, amendment of life, and the righteousness bestowed by God—will actually celebrate the feast of the kingdom. Guests who are there under false pretenses will be separated out. Their fate will be as bad, or worse, than those who originally refused to come to the feast. "Outer darkness" means, of course, judgment and its consequences. While it is true that Mt in this story is very hard on those who refuse the invitation, we note that he is even harder on those who come in and do not live up to the terms of belonging.

A major theme of Mt's gospel is the importance of living faithfully, according to the requirements of the God of Jesus Christ. The Sermon on the Mount (Mt 5-7) and the Parable of the Last Judgment (Mt 25:31-46) are examples. In the latter parable the final verse says that those who fail will go away into eternal punishment. "Outer darkness" is another way of saying the same thing. The Parable of the Wheat and the Tares (Mt 13:24-30) is particularly close to ours, a parable found only in Mt. In it the tares or "weeds" (as the RSV translates) sown in a field by an enemy are allowed to grow with the wheat "until the harvest," when they will be burned. To Mt's readers, "harvest" surely suggested the last judgment, and "burned" the eternal punishment, or "outer darkness."

We come now to the third way in which Mt changes the original thrust of the Parable of the Great Feast. He has placed it in the context of Jesus' controversies with his opponents in the temple, following his entry into Jerusalem.

In this passage (Mt 21:12—23:39) Jesus' confrontation with those who oppose him comes to its climax; he takes on in turn the chief priests, the elders, the Pharisees, the Sadducees, and the scribes. Throughout the passage, there are repeated reports that these groups sought to oppose him in every possible way. The passage ends with a long section (Mt 23:13-36) in which Jesus pronounces woes on his opponents. The tone is highly polemical throughout.

In this setting Mt's fierce version of the Parable of the Great Feast pronounces judgment on Jesus' opponents, who are the "murderers" who kill the servants (the Christian evangelists). They are themselves killed and Jerusalem, their city, is destroyed.

Particularly instructive for the interpretation of the Parable of the Great Feast is the Parable of the Wicked Tenants which precedes it (Mt 21:33-41). In this story, a householder clearly represents God, as does the king in the Parable of the Great Feast. The householder sends two sets of servants to his tenant farmers to get some of the produce, as the king sends two sets of servants to call the invited guests. In both parables, the two sets of servants surely represent God's witnesses. In both parables, the servants are mistreated and killed by those to whom they are sent.

A son also figures in both parables—more prominently in the Parable of the Wicked Tenants, where he is killed, an obvious allusion to the crucifixion. In both parables, the offending parties are rejected and others are given the reward they should have received.

It is difficult to believe that Mt has not edited both parables so that they make a pair; they are to be read together. The Parable of the Great Feast reinforces the Parable of the Wicked Tenants. Mt's readers could hardly read the former without having the latter in mind.

What conclusions can we draw from our examination of the changes Mt has made in the Parable of the Great Feast? When Mt responds to Jesus' invitation to join the conversation, the parable becomes something quite different from the original story told by Jesus. Gone is the metaphor-story based on ordinary life, and used to picture the kingdom. In its place Mt puts an elaborate allegory about God's relations to Jews, the chosen people, and to the new church. Gone is the sharp contrast between those who go about their business as usual and those who accept the challenge of Jesus' call to the kingdom banquet *now*. In its place Mt puts animosity between the host and the invited guests so drastic it leads to war. Gone is the simple fact that anyone available and willing can be brought into the kingdom banquet. In its place Mt puts a decisive shift in attention, away from the originally invited guests to those who were brought in later—and to one guest in particular.

At the same time, the original version of the parable has made its impression on Mt. He has picked up and intensified the theme of judgment that was certainly there in Jesus' original telling. The rejection of those who refused the invitation, which Mt makes much of, also appeared in Jesus' version. Both Jesus and Mt allow that anyone who wants to come can come, and they both tell the parable in terms which make unmistakably clear the *corporate* character of the kingdom. On what other basis could Mt include the destruction of an entire city? Our response to this destruction, a response also found in the Bible, is to ask why a city should be punished for what some of its citizens did. It is a fair question, but it should not obscure the point that Jesus and Mt stand

44

together against most of us in their understanding of the kingdom as a corporate, not individual, reality.

The parable as Mt received it proves somewhat awkward as a vehicle for his message. A war undertaken while a banquet awaits is bizarre. Moreover, the parable as Jesus told it does not allow Mt to focus attention on those brought into the banquet without his addition of the Parable of the Wedding Garment. Why then did he use it? Probably because the story was in his sources and its presence there was an invitation, a challenge; it called for response. The response is surprising. How did Mt get from the version he received to the notion of using it as he did? We do not know, but we can imagine Mt pondering this parable in his own situation, asking himself how best to enter into the conversation. We can be sure that Mt's own situation provided the pressure on him to use the parable as he did. He asked, "Does it help us to tell the story *this way*?" His version of the story is meant to address his own contemporaries.

Mt's Readers Respond

How would Mt's readers have understood the parable? It will help at this point to ask what sort of readers these were. To what community did Mt write? Careful work on the whole of Mt's gospel, examining his use of his sources, his own additions and changes in the material, his editing and arranging of his stories, suggests the following: Mt wrote sometime between the years 80-95 C.E. to a Jewish Christian community under heavy pressure, probably persecution, from the surrounding Jewish community. By this time the division between Jews and Christians had become a sharp one in Mt's community, although not everywhere else. The two communities stood over against each other, each claiming to be the true Israel and denouncing the other.

The ferocity of the Parable of the Great Feast and the strong polemic in the surrounding passages (Mt 21:12–23:39) suggest that the dominant group in Mt's milieu was composed of non-Christian Jews, and that their opposition to the Jewish Christian group was very strong, even violent. A number of indications elsewhere in the gospel support this notion, and in this gospel, Jesus often warns his followers of persecution to come. The Parable of the Wedding Garment, as well as other material in the gospel, indicates that from Mt's point of view his community was in some danger of falling short of its calling, and of failing to live out the righteousness God had given.

How then would Mt's readers have understood the Parable of the Great Feast? They would probably have noted without surprise the shift from a banquet to a marriage feast, from a host to a king. The preceding parable of the wicked tenants is clearly allegorical, so to have another allegory following immediately would not seem out of place. Mt's elimination of the three business-as-usual excuses for missing the banquet would not have caused any concern; a community sorely pressed by enemies all around is not in danger of lapsing into business-as-usual. The excuses probably would not have spoken with any power to Mt's readers. As for the two sets of servants, the readers would have recognized them from the preceding Parable of the Wicked Tenants as the witnesses to God's kingdom, mistreated for their proclamation.

The thrice-repeated statement that the banquet is ready might have been received by Mt's readers with some irony. *When?* they might have asked. Mt and his readers lived at a time when hopes for the coming of Christ in glory had dimmed. Some fifty years of waiting had taken their toll. Mt may have insisted on this point precisely because his church, under persecution, was experiencing discouragement and doubts. By repeating three times that the feast is ready, Mt has increased the urgency of the invitation and of the choice people had to make. The urgency was not, for Mt's readers, a question of having only a short period of time in which to answer the kingdom summons, but rather the urgent need for the church to stand fast in a situation of grave difficulty and danger.

Mt's church was a second-generation community. The period in which the earliest Christians had awaited the Lord's imminent return was coming to an end. The first generation of Christians, the apostles and those who had known Jesus in his earthly ministry, were gone. Mt's church was beginning to come to terms with

46

the possibility that the waiting period might be long. If that should prove to be the case, what would constitute faithfulness and obedience, especially in a situation of persecution? Mt's answer to this question is to insist that steadfastness and the exercise of righteousness are the calling of the Christian, especially since they do not know when the Lord will come. (See, for example, the parables in Mt 24:45–25:46). In the Parable of the Great Feast, Mt tells his readers that the lengthening of the waiting period does not mean that the banquet is not ready; it is indeed ready, but the originally invited guests have been found unworthy. They have refused to come. That is all the more reason for those who responded to the invitation to prove themselves worthy.

The notion that God destroyed Jerusalem by means of the Roman army because the Jews by and large did not accept Jesus as the Messiah, was not a new one to Mt's readers. For them, the king's action in this parable must have been a source of reassurance. The king does not abandon his servants to their mistreatment, but comes to their aid with swift and terrible retribution against the "murderers." His readers must have heard Mt say, "Take heart. God has not and will not desert you, the servants."

In contrast to this reassuring note, the unworthiness of the invited guests might have struck a somewhat different one. We wonder if Mt's readers could have escaped the doubts that assail a community under persecution. *Why* did Jews refuse, by and large, to accept Jesus as the long-promised and hoped for Messiah? Was he, in fact, the Messiah? Or were the Jews right and the Jewish Christians misled, deluded? Mt insists that such is not the case. Those who reject Jesus are themselves rejected. The division between those who believe the truth and those who do not begins now, and will be confirmed in the future. Mt's readers are those who have been called into the banquet of the kingdom of God.

Thus far, this violent version of the Parable of the Great Feast has been understood as reassurance and support by Mt's beleaguered readers. They may have jumped to attention when they read that those brought in are "both good and bad." The parable is now speaking about *them*. After they have heard the Parable of the Wedding Garment, the point becomes clear: your presence at

God's kingdom banquet is not guaranteed. Mt's readers already
know all about his insistence on a life totally worthy of God's
high calling. Mt's gospel is full of it. Indeed, by the time they
get to the Parable of the Great Feast, they may be tired of hearing
about it. The story of the wedding garment makes its point with
some subtlety, however. The offending person is addressed as
"friend." He represents them; he is one of those called into the
banquet. The guest is asked in a friendly way why he has not
lived up to his calling. And, we are told, he is speechless! For us,
this is an odd element in the parable, but not for Mt's readers. It
is like the Parable of the Last Judgement (Mt 25), "Lord, when
did we see thee. . . ." At the literal level the story makes no sense,
as we have noted, but the allegory is clear. If the garment is the
image of the way one lives and exercises one's calling, the man
with the improper garment finds out that it is too late. There is
nothing he can say. His "garment" speaks volumes. So he
receives the reward due to him, one even more terrible than that
inflicted on the guests who have rejected the invitation. Mt's
readers would not have been left in any doubt. They are being
told, "You have been called. Have you been chosen? That
depends on your faithful and consistent obedience to Jesus."

Modern Readers Respond

Modern readers are offended by the Parable of the Great Feast
as Mt has it. We see very clearly the identification of the king
with God. We are uneasy with the seemingly arbitrary and terrible
punishment given the man with the wrong garment. It may help
to know what the "garment" represents, and we may agree with
Mt that the way Christians live out their calling does make a difference. But we remain uneasy with this and with many other places
in Mt's gospel where believers are threatened with eternal punishment by a very demanding God. Where, in all of this, is the grace
of God, powerful enough both to forgive our inevitable lapses
and to provide us with the resources for transformation? What
has happened to "justification by grace alone?"

It should be said that one parable does not say everything, and that we need to read this one in connection with the many places where God's love and mercy are expressed in Mt's gospel. It is also well to note that in the New Testament it is Mt above all others who insistently calls Christians to the highest possible faithfulness and obedience to their calling. Our righteousness, it is clear in Mt, is given by God. Eternal punishment, so prominent in his gospel, is the consequence of turning away from God, a result that is not at all inevitable.

Modern readers are perhaps more offended by the parable because it pictures God destroying a city and its people. As children of our own age, we reply that the Romans destroyed Jerusalem and we want to say, "Don't blame it on God!" The parable's description of God is certainly not the one we associate with Jesus' teachings—although one reason this is so is that we tend to pick and choose which teachings we will take as typical. We are uneasy about the anti-Jewish sentiment so clearly expressed in the parable and in the material surrounding it. What has happened to "Love your neighbors," or more to the point, "Love your enemies?"

It is well to face the fact squarely that when Mt joins the conversation, he adds things that we do not like, that we want to push away. The parable does not say the same thing in every context. Each voice in the conversation is not one with which we will agree. We can allow Mt his place in the conversation and appreciate his contribution to the community to which he wrote. We are not compelled to like or agree with what he says. Where everyone agrees, there is no conversation.

We are certainly not compelled to imitate his voice when we join the conversation. It has been almost nineteen hundred years since Jews persecuted Christians. Since then, it has been the Christians who have persecuted the Jews. Given his hard line on the persecutors of his own day, one can imagine how hard Mt would be on those of today.

LUKE'S VERSION

We turn with relief from Mt to Lk's version of the Parable of the Great Feast. Here we meet Jesus as we know and revere him. Jesus in this parable is obviously concerned with the poor and unfortunate, concerned to include all who will come to the banquet. Moreover, a glance at Lk's version makes clear that he has stayed much closer to his source than Mt has. There are, however, some surprises for anyone who looks carefully at what is in the text.

Lk has changed the impact of the story as reconstructed in Q in two ways. First, he has altered the parable itself. Second, he has set it in a context which affects the way it is read and understood in his gospel. What do these changes tell us about Lk's understanding of the parable? We will look at the two ways he has used the parable.

First, Lk has made the following alterations in the parable itself:

a.   He has put the reference to the kingdom of God in the mouth of one of Jesus' dinner companions.
b.   The servant is sent out to call the guests "at the time of the banquet."
c.   The servant is sent to the "streets *and lanes of the city*."
d.   Those brought in are specified as "the poor and maimed and blind and lame."
e.   The servant, having done as bidden, reports to his master that "still there is room."
f.   The servant is sent out a second time, now into the "highways and hedges."

The first change, putting the reference to the kingdom of God in the mouth of a dinner companion of Jesus, is in part surely a simple editorial device to connect this parable with the preceding material. However it also shifts the center of attention from the preceding material to consideration of the kingdom.

Q

The kingdom of God is like a man who gave a banquet and sent his servant to call the invited guests, saying, "Come, for all is now ready." But they all alike began to make excuses. The first said to him, "I have bought a field, and I must go and see it; I pray you, have me excused." And another said, "I have bought five yoke of oxen, and I go to examine them; I pray you, have me excused." And another said, "I have married a wife, and therefore I cannot come." So the servant came and reported this to his master. Then the householder was angry and said to his servant, "Go out into the streets and invite as many as you find, and compel people to come in, so that the banquet hall will be filled. For none of those men who were invited shall taste of my banquet.

THE PARABLE OF THE GREAT FEAST —
LUKE'S VERSION
Lk 14:15-24

14: 15 When one of those who sat at table with him heard this, he said to him, "Blessed is he who shall eat bread in the kingdom of God!" 16 But he said to him, "A man once gave a great banquet, and invited many; 17 and at the time for the banquet he sent his servant to say to those who had been invited, 'Come; for all is now ready.' But they all alike began to make excuses. The first said to him, 'I have bought a field, and I must go out and see it; I pray you, have me excused.' 19 And another said, 'I have bought five yoke of oxen, and I go to examine them; I pray you, have me excused.' 20 And another said, 'I have married a wife, and therefore I cannot come.' 21 So the servant came and reported this to his master. Then the householder in anger said to his servant, 'Go out quickly to the streets and lanes of the city, and bring in the poor and maimed and blind and lame.' 22 And the servant said, 'Sir, what you commanded has been done, and still there is room.' 23 And the master said to the servant, 'Go out to the highways and hedges, and compel people to come in, that my house may be filled. For I tell you, none of those men who were invited shall taste my banquet.' "

The phrase "at the time of the banquet" was probably added because Luke was writing to a Gentile and urban audience who might not have known about the Jewish custom of two invitations—one in advance and one when the dinner was in fact ready. By his addition, Lk has brought his readers along with him into a time and place alien to them.

The command to go out into the "streets and lanes" and to the "highways and hedges" may be an example of Lk's imitation of the style of Old Testament writing, where so often things are said twice. This kind of repetition is often done in poetry; one has only to glance at the psalms. It is also characteristic of many Jewish writings. The double identification may also be for emphasis; that is, it calls Lk's readers' attention to the *places* the servant was sent. A more important clue to the same point is the addition "of the city." The first mission of the servant was to the people of the city; the second ("highways and hedges") is clearly to those outside the city. We will return to this point below.

Lk specifies those to be brought in as the poor, the maimed, the blind, and the lame. No reader could miss the point: it is the unfortunates, those who would never get invited to such a party, those who lived marginal existences, who are invited. In this connection we note that in the material which precedes this parable (Lk 14:12-14), Jesus instructs his dinner companions to invite exactly these folk, not their own well-to-do friends, when they give a party. The original parable did not specify who was to be brought in; in changing it, Lk makes a sharp point about appropriate kingdom behavior. Those who will be included in the kingdom banquet are those whom you must invite now.

There is an important tension in Lk's version of the parable which we must not lose sight of. That is the tension between the two statements, "Come, for all is now ready" and "Still there is room." The urgency of the first statement is mitigated by the second. Lk, writing sometime at the end of the first century, after the death of the apostles and the first Christian generation, knew that the "too late" implied in the original parable had not yet come. There was still time; the Gentile mission was in full swing and making great strides. Clearly, there was still time for people to respond to the call and come in. So Lk added the statement,

"And still there is room." What is interesting to note is that he did not take out the first statement, but the two are allowed to stand in tension with each other in one story. Lk is not trying to erase the previous parable. He is joining the conversation.

Once we notice that point, Lk's mention of the two places where the servant went to find people become understandable. The "city" surely represents Judaism; the "outside," the Gentiles. By extending the second invitation to the "others" found in the "highways and hedges," Lk speaks of the two missions of the early church. His Gentile readers would not have missed the reference to themselves, as those who were brought in from "the highways and hedges."

So it appears that Lk, like Mt, has turned the parable into an allegory at this one point. Those brought into the banquet represent the two missions of the church, Jewish and Gentile. In this connection, we note that the latter group are to be "compelled" to come in. We assigned this comment earlier to Jesus' version of the parable because it is consistent with the modes of courtesy of Jesus' time and place. It is now possible to see a further reason for assigning it to Lk's source, rather than to Lk himself. It is clear that Lk would not want to add the word "compel," with its undertone of coercion and its suggestion that God compels people to come into the kingdom. There is no suggestion elsewhere in Lk's work that he wants to emphasize such a notion. In fact, the word "compel" does not contribute to Lk's purposes in the use of the parable. Why then does he include it? Why not eliminate it? Again, it is not Lk's purpose to obscure his source. He allows the word to stand because he is joining the conversation, not trying to eliminate another's voice.

The final verse in Lk's version, "For I tell you, none of those men who were invited shall taste my banquet," is also the ending we chose for our reconstruction of the source, rather than Mt's ending. It is now possible to see why. Lk's has a two-fold focus in this parable. First, he identifies as the outcasts and marginal people those invited in from the streets. Second, he extends the invitation to those outside the city, the Gentiles. Lk is interested not so much in the originally invited guests who refuse to come, but in those who were later brought in. It is highly unlikely, then that he would add a comment at the end of the parable which directs his readers *back* to the originally invited guests. It is much more likely that the comment stood in his original source and that he concluded his parable, after making changes, as his source has concluded it. Lk is not interested in obliterating the voice which has come to him; he is interested in joining the conversation.

Having looked at the ways Lk has altered the parable we turn to the question of context. How has Lk changed the impact of the parable by the setting he has given it in his gospel? As we noted earlier, it is a friendly setting: Jesus is at dinner with a ruler-Pharisee host and others. Our parable comes at the end of a series of three paragraphs which have dinners as a common theme. This material is designed to instruct Lk's church on how they are to live, how they are to behave. The teaching proceeds in an interesting way. First, the readers are urged to practice humility, in 14:7-11, the famous passage where they are told not to take the best seats first, lest they then be demoted. This is routine ethics, typical of Judaism and other religions; it is also shrewd advice on how to avoid being humiliated. Second, the readers are told to give their parties for the outcasts (14:12-14). By itself, this story is mildly repellent. A rich man is to give large dinner parties to which he condescendingly invites those who would never dream of being invited. The host would be generous, yes, but nothing really changes except that the poor get one good meal. The host is still the powerful, though benevolent one; the poor are still powerless. Like the advice on humility, this too is quite routine, typical morality voiced by the pious of all faiths.

Someone at the table picks up on Jesus' words about the reward for such behavior ("You will be repaid at the resurrection of the just") and changes the subject. Instead of routine piety and morality, he speaks about the joyous celebration to be had in the hoped-for kingdom. Jesus, in Lk's version, here introduces a sharp reversal. It is only when his readers have read the Parable of the Great Feast that they will understand the statement in Lk 14:11, "For everyone who exalts himself will be humbled and he who humbles himself will be exalted." The kingdom banquet is for outcasts. To take a lowly seat at the party, to invite the poor to your dinners, is not at all routine morality when read together with the Parable of the Great Feast. What if it is literally true that the kingdom is for the poor? To take that seriously, to live it out in one's life, would upset a lot more than a few dinner parties.

What conclusions can we draw from our examination of the changes Lk made in the Parable of the Great Feast? When Lk responds to Jesus' invitation to join the conversation, the echoes of the parable as Jesus told it and as Lk received it are strong. The changes Lk has made are fewer and less drastic than those made by Mt; still, those changes are significant. The parable becomes, in Lk's hands, both a moral example story and an allegory of the church's two missions. Gone is Jesus' emphasis on the need to decide for the kingdom *now*. In its place are Lk's words, "Still there is room." Gone is the completely open invitation to anyone who will come in, as Jesus told the parable. Instead, the poor and unfortunate are specified. These are subtle but far-reaching changes, made by Lk under the pressures of the church's needs in his own time and situation. Concern for marginal people, so prominent everywhere in Lk's gospel, is also evident here. Jesus' parable speaks of bringing in just anyone from the streets, and the picture of those in the banquet hall is thus a very mixed and comic one. The hearer imagines a gathering that simply does not happen in the normal course of events: rich and poor, law-abiding and negligent, well-scrubbed and grimy, farmers, artisans, shopkeepers, the unemployed, all rubbing elbows at the same dinner table. Lk's picture, which is the one most of us carry around, is more *limited* than Jesus'. At Lk's dinner table one finds only the poor and un- fortunate and the foreigners. This also is an odd mixture, a strik- ing one, but it is not the same one that Jesus pictured.

Lk's second major change in the parable is more drastic, his addition of the phrase "And still there is room." The result is a sharp tension between that statement and "Come, for all is now ready." The warning in Jesus' parable, that those who exclude themselves and go about their lives on a business-as-usual basis will find that they are *too late*, is really undercut in Lk's parable. Indeed, the parable is an odd and awkward vehicle to carry this part of Lk's message. Why use a parable which speaks about the urgency of coming to the kingdom banquet *now*, if your message is that there is still time to bring others in? The reason Lk delivers this message is clear: the sense of urgency caused by the expectation that Jesus would soon return as Lord was beginning to wane. Like Mt, Lk lived in a period when the church was learning to come to terms with the delay of the Lord's return. So there is no mystery about Lk wanting to say, "Still there is room." But why use a parable which says just the opposite of what you want to say? Perhaps because the parable that Lk's readers know says "Come, for all is now ready," and encourages precisely those expectations which Lk and his church know have not yet been fulfilled. For their time and place, something needs to happen to the parable if it is to continue to speak with power to the church. Lk joins the conversation in order to offer an alternative.

Lk's Readers Respond

How would Lk's readers have heard and understood the parable? We can first summarize the scattered comments above about who these people were. Careful study of the whole of Lk's gospel and his second volume, The Acts of the Apostles, suggests that Lk wrote to a largely Gentile community without close ties to Judaism or Jewish Christians. Lk wrote everywhere in a way which seemed designed to draw this community into relationship both with the Old Testament and with the Judaism out of which Jesus and the earliest church sprang. It was a relatively affluent church, or a least had some affluent members, a conclusion suggested by Lk's concern everywhere for the poor and unfortunate. It is a second-generation church; that is, a church, like Mt's, which existed after the time of the apostles and the earliest followers of Jesus, a church learning to come to terms with the delay of the expected return of the Lord.

How would such people have heard the Parable of the Great Feast? They would have noted with interest Lk's setting for the story: Jesus is at dinner with a Pharisee ruler and his friends. This might have been surprising, as Lk's readers knew the Pharisees to be Jesus' opponents, although there are other places in Lk's gospel where the Pharisees are occasionally pictured as friendly, as in Lk 13:31. They would have heard the two teachings of Jesus

about humility and about inviting the poor and unfortunate to
their dinner parties, which precedes this parable, and these teachings typical of the early church would have come as no surprise.
His readers would have also known by this time that Lk designed
his gospel to highlight Jesus' concern for the poor and outcast.

The readers would certainly have noticed the shift caused by
the exclamation of one of Jesus' dinner companions, "Blessed is
the one who will eat bread in the Kingdom of God." This is a
new lead-in to the parable as they knew it in the Q version. This
new twist might alert them to expect a word from Lk that would
address their need to make adjustments, given the delay in the
Lord's return. The beginning of the parable, however, does not do
this; it is still the parable they know, complete with "Come, for
all is now ready." Hearing again the excuses of those who refuse
to come, as well as the host's justifiable anger at their refusal, Lk's
readers might have asked themselves, "Do we do that? Do we go
about our business as usual in the face of Jesus' call? How can we
do otherwise when we have learned the hard way that the banquet
is long delayed?"

A partial answer to their question comes with Lk's identification of those brought in off the streets, the outcasts. They would
not miss the fact that the list is the same as in the previous
account of those whom they are to invite to their dinner parties.
So *these* are the ones brought into the kingdom banquet! Is Lk
claiming a link between what we do now and our participation in
the kingdom banquet? We are kind to the poor not as a benevolent compassionate community, of which there are many, but
because *God* has chosen them. The outcasts are the first to be
brought into the banquet hall. They take precedence; they are
brought into the center of things. Perhaps Lk is addressing a
church in which the poorer and less fortunate members of the
community itself were being treated as unimportant and marginal.
Lk's parable may have addressed the more affluent of his readers
in a much more pointed way than we usually discern. For Lk,
Christian faithfulness to Jesus' proclamation of the kingdom,
however far off that kingdom may be, means putting the poor
and unfortunate first.

Then, after returning from the streets and lanes of the city,

58

the servant reports that there is still room in the hall. His master tells him to go outside the city to bring in others. Does that mean, Lk's readers might have wondered, that he is going to include us and address us after all? They certainly understood those outside the city to be themselves. They have been brought in and still the banquet hall is not full. The statement, "And still there is room," describes their situation. The warning of the parable, that if one does not come now it will be too late, has been mitigated. Lk's readers heard the host's instruction addressed to them: "Compel people to come in." The kingdom banquet is ready, but it will not be eaten until the intention of the host is fulfilled—until the house is filled. That time has not yet come. The present is the time for mission.

The final comment of the parable, "None of those men who were invited shall taste of my banquet," was familiar to Lk's readers. Perhaps after hearing Lk's version some of them had the wit to see that they might be the ones who made excuses, who continued business as usual. If that is so, Lk calls them to mission while there is still room.

Modern Readers Respond

As modern readers, we are much more comfortable with Lk's version of the Parable of the Great Feast than with Mt's. In Lk we meet the Jesus we think we know, whose concern for the poor and the outcast we do not always emulate, but which we recognize and revere. We, like Lk, know that "still there is room." The mission of the church goes on and we are both those who have been called and those who extend the mission by our own witness. We would miss part of Lk's point, however, were we to overlook the fact that the original claim, "Come, for all is now ready," is still there. The command, "Come now," has not diminished in importance because the kingdom in its fullness has not yet come. For Lk and for us, now is always the time for witness and mission. Lk claims that the kingdom is for the unlikely, for the ones who do not appear to have the right credentials for entry. Where do we stand in relation to this kingdom?

CONCLUSION

Before turning from Mt and Lk to join the conversation ourselves, let us look at what we have done thus far. We have reconstructed something like a history of the parable, so that it is now possible for us to trace its development from Jesus' original telling to its versions in Mt and Lk. It is, of course, not a complete history of the parable, which was undoubtedly used in many situations of which we have no knowledge. However, we can see at least six stages. As noted in chapter one, there are not strictly chronological stages. They surely overlap at points (for example, the oral tradition stage and Q), and two or more may be roughly contemporaneous (for example, Mt's and Lk's version). We do not know when the version in the Gospel of Thomas took form.

In tracing the history of the parable, we have used diverse methods, each useful in reconstructing one layer of tradition. These methods prove to be dependent one on the other. That is, the reconstruction of any one layer of tradition will not be firm until all the methods have been used and the history of the parable (in so far as we can trace it) is complete. For example, to arrive at the source Q, we identified what is common to both Mt's and Lk's version. In doing so we noted echoes of Lk's three excuses, found in Mt, although the three excuses are absent in Mt. We concluded that the three excuses probably stood in the source Q. In the next step, we compared the reconstructed source Q with the typical form of oral story-telling and noted that such stories very often proceed by way of a three-fold motif. This confirmed our previous judgment that the three excuses in Lk come from earlier layers of tradition.

It is useful to summarize what we have done thus far before we turn to our own contributions to the conversation.

History of The Parable of the Great Feast: Stage One
When Jesus told the parable it sounded something like this:
The kingdom of God is like a man who gave a great feast and sent his servant to call the invited guests, saying, "Come, for all is now ready." But they all made excuses. The first said to him, "I have

bought a field, and I must go out to see it; I pray you, have me excused." And another said, "I have bought five yoke of oxen, and I go to examine them; I pray you, have me excused." And another said, "I have married a wife and therefore I cannot come." So the servant came and reported this to his master. Then the householder was angry and said to his servant. "Go out into the streets and invite as many as you can find and compel them to come in, that my house may be filled. For I tell you, none of these men who were invited shall taste my banquet.

Jesus told a comic story that makes fun of the invited guests and their excuses. The refusal of all the guests, leaving the host with a party to which no one will come, is unlike normal life. So also is his invitation to the motley crew from the streets. This parable about the kingdom left Jesus' listeners in no doubt: the kingdom was an unexpected reality. Their previous definitions of what it would be and who would get in were sharply challenged. Moreover, the decision to *come now* was imperative. The banquet hall was filling up and it would soon be *too late*. On the other hand, anyone—anyone at all—who would accept the invitation into this unexpected kingdom was welcome. The message of the parable conforms to and interprets Jesus' own carelessness about those with whom he ate, both the upper-crust (religiously and socially) and the outcast. The kingdom about which Jesus tells parables is the kingdom he celebrates at the table now.

Stage Two
In the telling and retelling of the parable by the earliest Christians, the version Jesus had told did not need revision. On the contrary, the little group of Jews who were convinced that Jesus, the crucified and risen one, was the Messiah long awaited by them and by their fellow Jews, were also certain that he would soon return in glory to establish the kingdom on earth. This Jesus, the unexpected Messiah, was still understood in the conventional terms of Jewish kingdom expectation. The unexpected, indeed, scandalous event of his death (the Messiah was not supposed to come and *die*) had been overcome in the resurrection and in God's pouring out of the Holy Spirit on those who believed in Jesus. To his followers, these events meant that the Messiah would surely soon

bring the kingdom. These early Christians truly heard Jesus' teaching about an unexpected kingdom, and truly believed that this unexpected Messiah was indeed God's Messiah. It is interesting to note, however, that they understood all of this in terms of the conventional, traditional kingdom expectations. They still expected the risen and exalted Messiah to come in glory soon to establish the visible kingdom on earth. Consequently, the parable as Jesus told it was useful to them. They told and retold it as they proclaimed the message: this Jesus, crucified and risen, will soon come to bring the kingdom banquet. Come in now, before it is too late.

Stage Three
The hypothetical source Q included the parable in its collection of stories about Jesus' ministry as the story had been told orally. Its inclusion in Q involved two changes in the thrust of the parable. First, it was translated into Greek from the original Aramaic and therefore made available to a wider audience, probably the Greek-speaking Jews of the Mediterranean world, of whom there were hundreds of thousands. Second, by reading the parable as part of a *collection* of stories, readers had at their fingertips a number of Jesus' parables and teachings about the kingdom of God. The parable was augmented by others that filled out the teaching of Jesus and the earliest church on the character of the kingdom. The main points of this parable—that its hearers must change their traditional ideas about the kingdom and that the urgent requirement was to decide now—stood together with teaching about other issues.

Stage Four
The community which produced the Gospel of Thomas knew a version of the parable similar to that of Q. Gnostic Christian communities, which date from very early in the church's life, were a diverse lot and we obscure the realities if we describe them in too limited ways. It is possible to say, however, that by and large they despised normal human enterprises, such as earning one's living, as activities that dragged the spirit down and made spiritual progress toward the divine impossible. Someone in the

group used the parable to speak in typically Gnostic terms: the bias against commerce and all kinds of business is the most obvious. It is easy to see how the three excuses, with a fourth one added, can be altered slightly in order to have Jesus speak against ordinary commerce.

Stage Five

Mt wrote at the end of the first century and used the parable to address his contemporaries. He and they lived in a setting of severe conflict with Judaism, which itself emerged from the Jewish war much changed from the Judaism of Jesus' time. Two major concerns are evident. First, Mt employs the parable as an allegory of God's dealings with the Jews; their refusal to accept Jesus as the promised Messiah has brought about the destruction of their city and their temple. The parable is part of a polemic against the Jewish rivals and opponents of Mt and his church.

Second, Mt addressed his community with a sternness equal to his attitude toward the enemy. The judgment of God evident in the destruction of Jerusalem would be visited also on any who, having accepted Jesus as Messiah, did not live out the greater righteousness required of his followers.

Stage Six

Lk, also writing at the end of the first century and using the parable to address his contemporaries, shifted the focus of the parable sharply away from the originally invited guests to those brought in from the "streets and lanes of the city" and from the "highways and hedges." Two major concerns emerged. The first was that those brought in off the streets were designated as the poor and crippled, the marginal. Lk answered the question of how the community was to live in the present, while it awaited the kingdom banquet. In a situation where the church was coming to terms with the fact that the wait may be a long one, Lk offered kingdom-related counsel. The kingdom is meant for the outcasts; these are the first to be brought in. That is why, in the passage immediately before this parable, Lk's readers were told to invite the outcasts to their parties. To live as a member of the future kingdom meant to take seriously Jesus' message that the kingdom was for them. Lk's readers were also to take their stand with the outcasts.

But what of the period of waiting itself? Lk's second major concern is expressed in the servant's words to his master, "Still there is room." Not all of those to be brought into the banquet hall had yet entered. The mission of the church continued. How do we live while we await the banquet? We carry on with the mission of the church.

Review of the Methods used in the Study

What questions have we asked in order to find and evaluate the evidence for tracing the development of the parable? First, and most important, we have worked from the two texts themselves. We have not begun with a general description of parables or with a theology of the kingdom or even with our notions about Jesus, and then used these to explain the parable. Instead, we have asked questions and sought evidence to account for the two versions of the parable which lie before us in the Bible.

Second, we have taken seriously the fact that the parable is part of *written* documents. We have asked questions about the literary characteristics of the accounts: which elements in the two versions are common to each other, and which are unique to one author? Where have the authors placed the parable in their larger works?

Third, we have asked about the oral story which stands behind our two written versions. What is the *form* of the oral parable? Are our written versions true to this form? In addressing the material in this way, we have been able to reconstruct the oral version of the parable.

Fourth, we have tested the oral reconstruction to see whether Jesus told it by asking four separate questions of the text.

1. Do we know this parable in more than one early source?
2. Does the parable conform to what we know of Jesus' own setting?
3. Is the parable distinct in its message both from the Judaism

64

of Jesus' time and from the interests and concerns of the early
post-resurrection church?
4. Does the parable conform to other reliable information we
have about Jesus?

At each stage of the parable, we have asked *historical* questions. How was the image of the banquet used in Jesus' time?
What were the Jewish expectations for the kingdom of God?
What were the customs related to giving dinner parties? What was
the impact of the Jewish-Roman war on the early Christians? In
seeking answers, we have gone first to our authors, Mt and Lk,
then to other New Testament material, then to the Jewish literature of the time of Jesus and the earliest church, then to the Old
Testament. Modern ideas about the Bible have informed our
study as instruments to uncover the first century realities; they
have not determined in advance our understanding of those realities. This does not mean that our own notions and reactions have
been absent in the study. It means that in this conversation we
have tried first to listen to voices other than our own.

Through our focus on the text and on related material we
have made contact with the human experience of the people who
told and wrote, heard and read, this story. We have begun to
answer questions. What did it feel like to listen to Jesus? To be
part of the church some years after he taught? What was at stake
for those people? How did they deal with their problems? We
have tried to allow Jesus and the early Christian communities to
be themselves, concretely, in their own time and place. The result
has been not only to resolve the apparent conflict between the
two versions of the story, but also and more important, to begin
to see concretely something of Jesus' original impact on his
listeners and some of the ways the earliest Christians used their
memories of him in their own settings.

When we join the conversation, we are both grateful to, and
troubled by, Mt's and Lk's versions of the Parable of the Great
Feast. In our better moments, we are grateful to Mt for raising
the question of God's judgment in such sharp tones. The judgment of God is, after all, part and parcel not only of teaching
about the kingdom in the New Testament, but of the whole of

the Bible and of the church tradition that follows. The Christian must sooner or later come to terms with it. We are also grateful for Mt's clearly corporate picture of the kingdom, which challenges our individualistic notions. Both these elements offer us a challenge.

We are troubled by the strong anti-Jewish sentiments in Mt's treatment of the parable. Most of us do not believe that God's relation to the world is as Mt pictures it. When we read of Mt's king who "sent his troops and destroyed those murderers and burned their city," we want to say that this is not the way God relates to the world. Mt might reply to our objection in the following way: "Very well. Then you tell *me* how God is related to the world. The kingdom is after all a political term, a term related to power and its exercise in the world. If God's kingdom does not mean that God is related to the world as I have it, what is the relationship? The kingdom means nothing if it does not mean the exercise of God's power in the world."

We have the same mixed reaction to Lk's version of the parable, although in this case our gratitude probably outweighs our unease. We are grateful to Lk because he shares our view of the kingdom expectation. We, too, know that "still there is room," and we do not know quite how to respond to all the New Testament talk about how Jesus will return soon. Two thousand years is not "soon" on anyone's calendar. If we take seriously the corporate, this-worldly character of the kingdom as it is reflected in all of the stages of the parable, we do not see much in the world that tells us God's kingdom is gaining over the forces which oppose it. There is a story about the rabbi who was told that the Messiah had come. He looked out of the window and said, "I do not see that the world is any different." The rabbi had a point. To be told by Lk that "still there is room" gives us a biblical basis for what we know to be true: the kingdom has not yet come. Lk might reply to this, "Very well. But do not overlook the fact that the other statement is also in my version of the parable, 'Come, for all is now ready.' Earlier generations of Christians may have been too quick to draw the conclusion that the kingdom would be established immediately, but if that conviction was wrong, we must pray and ponder about what a better interpreta-

66

tion of Jesus' kingdom message might be. If we do not struggle seriously with his words about the kingdom, we will lose his message."

We are both grateful to and troubled by Lk's designation of those brought into the feast as the "poor and maimed and blind and lame." On the one hand we know that we need to be reminded of our obligations as Christians to care for the outcasts. On the other hand we are uneasy about the suggestion that the kingdom is only for them. This was not the case in the parable as Jesus told it; there, anyone at all who would come was welcome. We speak, admittedly, with a bias, for by and large we are not the poor and unfortunate. Are we also welcome in the kingdom, according to Lk? Lk might reply to our comments this way: "My readers knew the version that said anyone who would come was welcome. That is fine. But there is more. When a message like that is told and retold, people get used to hearing it and they become complacent. If the parable is to continue to speak with power in the churches, it must say something which will jolt its listeners awake again. It was clear to me in my situation that my fellow Christians did not connect their invitation to be part of the kingdom with the fact of Jesus' ministry to the poor. So I believed they needed reminding in very sharp terms. The kingdom expectation must not be allowed to recede into the background of our lives; it must be reinterpreted so that it speaks to the center of things."

We are both grateful to and troubled by both Mt and Lk, taking their work on this parable together. We are grateful because they call us to work on the parable, to be active in our endeavor to put ourselves in touch with Jesus. We are intrigued by the fact that they chose to write their messages in the form of gospels, thus keeping the memories of Jesus close to the life of their churches. We are humbled by the fact that their works are anonymous, by their apparent lack of interest in being identified as individuals, their desire to stand with their readers instead of over against them as authorities. Mt and Lk free us to engage them in conversation, as we see them in conversation with their own communities. We are interested in their strange combination of respect for their material and at the same time their freedom with it. Their stance encourages us to take a similar one.

At the same time, we confess our irritation with them for changing the stories. We have questions to put to them that they do not answer. We have a question for ourselves that they do not seem to be concerned with, namely, in what sense is Scripture authoritative? What are we to do with this conglomeration of layers of tradition we have before us in their gospels? In what sense is Scripture *true*? Mt and Lk, who often disagree with each other, might respond this way, with one voice, "Scripture? What Scripture? We were not writing Scripture. When we wrote, we addressed our own communities. If your church later made us into part of the Bible, the problem is not ours! But if we are Scripture for you, you might do well to look at the way we worked. Look at the respect we had for the tradition we received and the freedom we had in dealing with it. We are convinced that we were called by God and inspired by the Holy Spirit to do the work we did. Does our work not offer you some clues about how you might use your Scripture in order to address the church in your own time?"

68

3.

We Join the Conversation

> I would like to have the men of Heaven in my own house;
>   with vats of good cheer laid out for them.
> I would like to have the three Marys, their fame is so great.
> I would like people from every corner of Heaven.
> I would like them to be cheerful in their drinking.
> I would like to have Jesus sitting here among them.
> I would like a great lake of beer for the King of Kings.
> I would like to be watching Heaven's family
>   Drinking it through all eternity.
>   St. Brigid, 10th c.

The conversation we enter has many voices, including all those who have responded to the parable over the centuries from Mt's and Lk's time to our own. We begin with the tenth century poem above because it is an excellent example both of respect for the parable's story and freedom in relation to it. The author has heard Jesus' note of rejoicing at the gathered banquet and offered her own note of humor and celebration. There is also a hint of wistfulness; she looks forward to a time when she can offer a "lake of beer" to the celebrants.

In this brief poem or song, the author not only evokes the parable for her listeners. She also recasts it completely, in a way that recreates it for her time and her contemporaries to give them a powerful vision of the celebration of the kingdom of God. In a few lines she has also included us in her world, we who read her words centuries after they were written and catch a glimpse of rejoicing and hope from another era.

As we join the conversation about the kingdom of God pictured in the Parable of the Great Feast, we do well to remember some of the characteristics of conversation and some of the demands it makes. Readers who have come this far have learned that a lot of patience is required. Others usually have more to say than we are willing to hear. Participation in a conversation demands openness and imagination if we are to listen to others as they wish to be heard. It also requires our own active participation. We will not only respond, but also raise our own questions and concerns.

The diversity of voices suggests that the result of a conversation will not be so much a solution or "right" answer to a problem as a sharing of possibilities. It will be an offering of ideas that will not only shed light on our subject, but also, and more important, provide us with power to move forward. Each participant asks, "Does it help us to tell the parable this way?" or "Does it help us to respond to the parable this way?"

As we join the conversation about the kingdom of God with Jesus and Mt and Lk, a number of factors influence us. One of these factors is the way our partners in conversation have made their points. Jesus told a comic parable that made people laugh as it made them think. Mt and Lk retold the parable with both respect for and freedom with the parable they had received. A mixture of humor, respect, and freedom may help us to join the conversation creatively.

Mt and Lk were involved in conversation with a double focus; they conversed both with Jesus and with their own contemporaries. We will surely want to do the same, to listen to Jesus and to our contemporaries. Unlike Jesus, we will not address our friends and neighbors with authority; rather we will, like Mt and Lk, ask which responses help us to get on with the business of living out the Christian life. We will not say what Mt and Lk said, for we face different problems. At the same time we will not turn away from what they said, nor try to smooth over the difficulties they pose, nor try to domesticate them.

To be in conversation about the kingdom of God is to speak about a difficult reality. The difficulties are several. First, many people think of the kingdom as an interior reality only. Second, the word "kingdom" itself reminds some people of a mythical place in fairy tales. Third, a kingdom is a geographical place, like the United Kingdom, so it is not a central image for people who live, as we do, in a constitutional democracy. Rather, it is clear from listening to Jesus, Mt, and Lk that for them the kingdom of God means God's exercise of power as king in the world.

There are other difficulties. We often think of the kingdom of God as a future reality, because the New Testament so often speaks of it that way. Since our world is very far from being a manifestation of the kingdom, many people find it difficult to believe that it will ever be a reality in this world. Life with God beyond death is for many the substitute for the biblical notion of the kingdom. For others, however, the tragedy and suffering endured by many people on earth requires a resolution, if we are to believe that God has something important to do with our lives now. It is not enough to view this vale of tears merely as a prelude to heaven. Why would God have sent Jesus to this world, if not to make a difference here? The full resolution of this-worldly life is an essential element in Christian faith. In Jesus' parable he speaks about the kingdom as a feast that is ready now. What can that mean for us who hear the parable two thousand years later?

The pieces that follow are contemporary responses to the Parable of the Great Feast. The play was performed by the children of the General Theological Seminary on December 7, 1982 during a celebration of the Eucharist. The other pieces were created as part of a New Testament course. After doing the kind of work on the parable found in the two earlier chapters, students were asked to make their own contributions to the conversation with Jesus, Mt, and Lk. No restrictions were made in regard to the form of each piece. One student painted a picture; another created a slide series of photographs she took in New York City. Many wrote sermons or outlines for group study of the parable, appropriate responses from people working in parishes and soon to enter the ordained ministry. The pieces included here were chosen because each one is a departure from the usual ways parables are used in our churches. They demonstrate in different ways both respect for and freedom with the parable.

I The Parable Retold by One of the Uninvited Guests
and
II The Parable Retold by One of the Invited Guests

by Teresa Payne

I

The rain had stopped, but it was cold that day, very cold. The
wind was blowing and pierced through our wet clothes, taking
away the little warmth we had. We were walking to keep warm.
I suppose we would have been walking in any weather. We were
trying to get to the city.

Our progress was slow. I had stepped into so many puddles
that my feet burned with the pain of the cold. The ground was
hard under my feet, and little stones kept digging into them. I was
so angry at the Mute for not leading me around the puddles I
hardly wanted to touch her. But I didn't have a choice. When I
had to depend on the Drunk to guide me I usually ended up in a
ditch—or worse. The Stupid One would forget who was leading
whom, so both of us got hurt. The Cripple had problems of his
own. So I was left with the Mute. She was surprisingly good, even
though she couldn't talk, and we were used to each other. But
lately she'd been coughing more and more; she just stopped paying
attention. At least she smelled better than the others.

The five of us made our way towards the city; there were
places there where it was warm, more than in the country. Food
was easier to come by, too. In the warm season the country was
better. That was our routine, winter in the city, summer in the
country. We were just like the idle rich. We were getting close,
the traffic on the road increased, and we began to pass the farms
owned by the rich city people. I could smell the earth that had
been turned after the harvest, and the bonfires burning the tares.

Early in the afternoon two men passed us on horseback. I
heard one saying to the other, "He gives great parties, always
about ten times more food than anyone could eat. But I've been
so busy lately I'd rather stay at home." The Drunk yelled out and

asked for baksheesh. The Stupid One called for help. The Mute
let go of my hand and ran up to the horses stretching her thin
arms towards the men. The Cripple waved his crutches in the air,
and I reached my hands out. It was a pathetic act, but it usually
worked. The only times people gave us anything were when they
felt really guilty. These men didn't even pause, they ran from us.
The Cripple came up to me. "How about you?" he asked. "Are
you too busy to eat? We could have lived for a month on what
his hat cost." "I could eat a hat today, if I had one." I told him.
For a while my anger made me warm.

We were hungry and getting hungrier. The wind got stronger
and it didn't help to keep moving, especially when we moved so
slowly. The Stupid One began to sing "Suppertime, suppertime,"
over and over, tunelessly. It got colder still, so I knew the sun
was setting. I carried the pack that held our food, but it was so
light I'd hardly been aware of it on my back. I think we were all
ready to give up for the night when the Mute began to tug on my
arm, and the Stupid One stopped singing. "It's the city! We can
see the city!" the Drunk yelled to me. "Maybe we can get a
drink." "A drink, some bread, some place out of the wind, I
don't care which," the Cripple said. Our spirits were lifted by the
possibilities in the city; we joined arms for the extra warmth and
walked a little faster.

It must have been at least a couple of hours more before we
were within the gates. When we got there the Drunk disappeared
right away. We knew he'd find us again, and we could eat his
share of the food until he did. We almost fell down in the first
alley, but within moments an old woman came up and started
hitting us with a stick. "I don't know where you're from, or who
you are, but get out! There isn't enough room here for all of us.
There is no food any where! Get out." It was the same story
wherever we went. Even on the streets the other beggars would
swear at us or commiserate with us. But the city was crowded,
all the usual places to camp in were filled, and there was no food
to be found anywhere. I was thinking that we would have been
better off in the farmland. Finally out of exhaustion we sat down
in a doorway.

It took almost no time to divide and eat the food we had; then there was a pause while we realized how hungry we still were, and come to grips with the fact that there would be no more food. The Stupid One began to cry softly. We huddled close together in the doorway and waited for someone to come tell us to move.

We must have fallen asleep. The next thing that happened was that someone was shaking us, telling us to wake up and asking if we were hungry. A number of rude comments came into my mind. I felt sick, and I ached all over, "This has gone on for too long." I thought. "I'm too tired to keep trying." Then what the man was saying penetrated my thoughts. There was food, somebody had food. The Mute grabbed my arm and we followed the man. Along the way he invited other street people, and soon we were a crowd. I heard snatches of his explanation. "No one would come . . . there's too much food for the household to eat in a month . . . he really wants someone to enjoy it."

I thought it was a dream, and then we went up some steps and into a large hallway, and it was warm. Then into another room that was even warmer. Somebody gave me a hot washcloth and I could wash my face and hands. There was sweet-smelling soap and soft towels. Somebody else took away my sodden rags and put soft slippers on my feet. A voice from inside the house was shouting, "Welcome, welcome, my friends!" I asked the Cripple if it was real and he said, "It is real, very beautifully real." Someone ushered us into another room that was huge and filled with the smells of food. Soft hands guided me to a chair and before I knew what had happened, I was eating, and eating.

II

Parties. I go to parties all the time. And I give parties, too. Granted, this particular host was the best. He had the most food, the most guests, the best entertainment and music. I liked his parties. And it wasn't just the quantities, there was something different about him, something special. I always left feeling good.

But it had been a tough few weeks. Although I had made a

lot of money I had worked hard doing it. I could hardly remember what my wife looked like. I hadn't taken the time to see my boys in ages. The only thing I'd taken time away from the business for was the temple. I still went regularly. One of my rabbi friends asked me why. I told him it was good for business. When things calmed down, I began to enjoy my social life again. I gave a big party and enjoyed the many invitations that came in return. It meant that I had a good time without much expense to me. In the midst of it all I got the invitation to the special host's party. It was a pleasant surprise. Naturally, I accepted.

One morning a few days later a friend came over and told me he knew a guy who was selling some land. It was just exactly the kind of deal I'd been waiting for. My friend didn't seem to think there was any rush, but I wanted that farm. I convinced him to take me out to meet the owner that afternoon. We were just walking out the door when the servant showed up telling us the big feast was ready for that night. I didn't know what to do. I had wanted to go to that party, but I wanted the land more. I looked over at my friend. If he found someone to buy the land, there was a good chance the owner would reward him and I would be in his debt, too. His fingers almost twitched as he mentally added up the drachmas. I took a coin out of my purse.

"Look," I said as I pressed it into the servant's hand. "Some rather crucial business has come up. It's urgent. You're going to have to excuse us." The servant looked me right in the eye without changing his expression at all. I began to feel uncomfortable, and my friend did, too. He got out a larger coin and gave it to the servant.

"Isn't it a shame," he said trying to be jocular. "We've been looking forward to this, but what can we do? Business is business." The servant bowed slightly and went out. With the excuse that it was cold outside, I offered my friend a drink. We had two and left for the country. On the way out we found the coins we had given to the servant. He had left them by the door.

We rode in silence for a while, and then began to gossip idly. Eventually we began talking about the party we had excused ourselves from. "I have to admit, he gives great parties, always about ten times more food than anyone could eat. But I've been so busy lately I'd rather stay at home tonight, once we get this business arranged. I've wanted a summer place for a long time. It's good for business. It attracts better people." My friend agreed.

In the middle of our conversation we passed a group of beggars. There were about five of them, an ugly, motley crew. I often throw them something, especially when there is a child. But this bunch looked worse than usual, sicker, dirtier, thinner. They made my skin crawl. We kicked our horses and got out of sight.

The farm was a disappointment. It was smaller and closer to town than I had expected. I didn't like the looks of the neighbors. Worst of all, the owner was asking far more than I was able to pay. We left, and feeling the cold much more than we had earlier, rode home quickly. My friend was very apologetic. He had embarassed me, and been a little embarassed himself by the owner of the house. I got to thinking about the beggars on the road, and then the party. When we got back to town, I asked my friend to come have a drink and join me for dinner.

I poured some wine and rang for a servant. But there was nothing prepared for dinner, we were not expected. The cook had gone out. The servant brought us what he could find, but there wasn't a lot. My wife only bought what she needed immediately. So we drank. We got very drunk, perhaps more than we meant to, I don't know. We swore at the owner of the house, and my cook, and suggested somebody get rid of the beggars cluttering up the streets, and wondered how the party was going. It wasn't until quite late that it suddenly occurred to me that we might still get in. We could pretend that the servant had misunderstood us, that we were only going to be late. We decided it was a good idea, and after another drink we pulled on our coats and made our way to the party.

If we hadn't been so drunk, we would have noticed that the house looked different. We could hear the music, and happy voices, but the windows were closed and covered by drapes and the door was shut. There were no carriages and no people coming and going. My stomach rumbled from hunger, and my head was reeling. I pulled my friend up the steps to the door with me. We knocked. There was no answer. We tried again, and still there was no answer. So we yelled and banged on the door and threw things at the windows. No answer. We banged and yelled together, "Let us in!" Finally we heard someone come to the door and unbolt it. It was the servant.

"I am sorry. The house is full; you are too late."

"But we were invited. Let us in."

"None of the guests who were invited are here. They made excuses, just as you did. Other people have taken your place." Just then I was able to see into the house, and I saw the beggars we had passed on the road, eating and singing. "I am sorry," the servant said. "You are too late." He closed the door and we were left alone on the steps. My friend had gotten very quiet and still. "I'm going home. I'll see you later," he mumbled and walked away. I too went home, and found we had finished the wine. My room was cold, the servants had gone to bed. I crawled under the blankets in my coat. I was very hungry.

In her retelling of the parable Teresa Payne heeds the sharp warning from Jesus that those invited must come when they are called, lest they be "too late." Those who rejected the original invitation try to come after all, but find they have excluded themselves from the party. She has also heard Luke's insistence on the poor and unfortunate as those who are to come in first. Luke would applaud her lack of sentimentality about these people, who are not pictured as "good" or "worthy," but as unfortunate and in need. There are poignant notes: the five help each other and what one cannot do, another can. The narrator is blind, a point we do not realize until we are well into the story. Luke would also approve the host's lack of paternalism; he does not condescend to them, but welcomes them as friends.

The first-person accounts from a member of each group answer to a need we have in understanding a parable from a long time ago and a milieu different from ours. While Jesus' listeners, and Mt's and Lk's readers, could fill in the pictures of the characters in the story from their own experience, here we are helped to do so. While the details of the contemporary story describe a

first-century setting, we have no difficulty in identifying with
them. The story-teller has offered us the opportunity to see ourselves in both her narrators.

The Forever Party

by Diane Corlett

" 'For I tell you, none of those men who were invited shall taste
my banquet.' " I closed the Bible and smiled my best pedagog-
ical smile at my five-year-old charge.
"What did you think of the story?"
She frowned in confusion. "But then what happened?"
I frowned in confusion. "What do you mean, 'then what
happened?' "
"What happened next? Who got to come to the banquet?
Didn't those first people get to come *ever*?"
"Uh, well. Let's see." I smiled, trying to stall for time. Ah!
I had it! "What do you think happened next?"
"I think that everybody got to come who wanted to, and the
person never ran out of food." She looked so earnest. And wise.
"You're probably right." This might be interesting. "Okay.
When that last servant came back with all those sick people who
wanted to come to the banquet, the party started. Everybody
sat down at a huge round table and the servants brought out all
kinds of food and drinks."
"What kind of food?"
"Whatever kind of special food each person needed to eat in
order to feel better." Sounded good to me. "What kind of food
makes you feel better?"
She thought for two seconds. "Spaghetti and chocolate
milk."
"Right. Well, as I said, everybody's food was special and
different. And the host had musicians who played beautiful,
soothing music that made everybody feel relaxed and happy."
"Did anybody dance or play games?"
"Oh, yes. Everyone who wanted to dance got up and
danced."

"Even the crippled people?"

"Especially the crippled people. They enjoyed the dancing very much. Even though they were still crippled, it didn't matter any more." I was on a roll. "They moved around as best they could because it made them happy. And their happiness seemed to make the host smile."

"What about the games?" She never forgets anything.

"People had races and threw darts and played all kinds of games. And the people who lost didn't mind a bit because it didn't matter."

"Because they were happy and the host was happy, so they were nice to each other and didn't cry when they lost."

"That's right. Very good thinking." We were really getting into the swing of this thing.

"What about the servants?" A curve.

"What about them?" A bunt.

"Did they get to eat, too?"

"Absolutely. After the sick people finished eating and relaxing they felt so good that they got up and let the servants sit down and they served the servants! They gave them the special food and drinks that they needed to make them feel good." A home-run.

"What about the musicians?"

"The musicians traded places with other guests as they finished eating, and the guests played music or sang for everybody else."

"What about the first people who didn't want to come?"

I hate that question.

"Well, they still didn't want to come. When the sick people had finished serving the servants they felt so much better, and so grateful to the host for having such a wonderful party, that they went out and invited other people to come to the banquet just as the first servants had invited them. And lots more people came to the party. Remember, we decided that the host never ran out of food? Well, he also wanted the banquet hall to be filled all the time. So, finally a sick person who felt better went to see the first people who were invited. She told them how kind the host was and how wonderful the party was, and how much better she felt since she had been to the party. But the people still didn't

want to come. One of them said that she was beginning to get a
headache, but that she was still too busy to come. The others
just went back to their jobs. So the sick person who felt better
kept going and found some other people who wanted to come to
the party, and she took them to the banquet with her and intro-
duced them to the host. Then she had them sit down and she
gave them their special food."

"They knew the host already."

"What?" I thought that she had been quiet too long.

"The sick people knew the host already or they wouldn't
have come to his party. Everybody knew him a little bit or they
wouldn't have come."

"Maybe so. Good thought."

"Since the host always has lots of food and he wants everybody to come, then those first people can come any time they
want. So don't worry. They know the host a little bit and they
might want to come later."

She looked so serious.

"Maybe you're right. Why do you think those people might
want to go to the banquet?"

"Everybody who goes to the party will go to them and invite
them to come, lots of times, until they finally want to come.
Then they will."

"Oh." Silence.

"What about the host?" I knew it.

"What about him?"

"Did he get to eat, too?"

"The host prepared the food and then he just enjoyed watching other people eat it. It was special food that was fixed just to
make the guests feel good."

"I know. But I eat food at my parties. I ate my birthday cake
last week." Clever child.

"That's true, but you didn't bake the cake. Your mother
baked it for you to enjoy. It was made especially for you to make
you feel good. And you shared your special cake with other
people who came to your party."

"It was a good party. Everybody sang and we played games.
And I got presents!"

"That's great! Did your mother eat the cake she baked?"
On-task question.

"No. She's on a diet."

"I see." So much for analogy.

"Why didn't you come to my birthday party?"

"I was at work. You know that. Remember, I brought you
a present after I got off work?"

"Yes, but my party was fun. You would have liked it. It
was like the banquet. Everybody was happy and we had special
food." She was upset.

"I'm sorry that I couldn't come. Maybe I can come next
year."

"It'll be different next year. I won't be five, I'll be six. It'll
be a different cake."

She frowned for a moment and then brightened.

"But you could still come." She smiled broadly with ever-
growing largesse. "I want everybody to come."

"Thank you. I'll be there."

We sat together for a moment in silence. She was sitting in
my lap with her head leaning back against my chest.

Not moving. "Is that party still going on?"

Silence. "How do you mean?"

"Like Christmas and like my birthday. They happen every
year, but I was only born one time and Jesus was only born one
time."

"Well, I guess the party is still going on. I guess that all the
people who have been to the party tell other people about it, and
they just keep going."

She patted the Bible which was stuck between the arm of the
chair and the cushion.

"Jesus told us about the party."

"That's true."

"Can we go to the party?"

"Yes, Baby." We snuggled closer and she stuck her thumb in
her mouth. "We're at the party now."

Diane Corlett gets her point across through a modern conversation about the ancient parable. She has noticed its accent on the kingdom of God as a celebration, which Jesus' listeners certainly understood, and Lk's emphasis on the poor and unfortunate. She has also voiced for the rest of us the uneasiness we feel about the original guests who refused to come; the child in the story is haunted by their exclusion. Is that why she wants to know if the servants and musicians got to be part of the celebration? The child insists they can still come, if only they will. But the author sticks with the original parable; those invited first still do not want to come, even when repeatedly pressed. They exclude themselves.

There is an interesting twist to this modern parable. Even though it is based on Lk's version, the story lacks any reference to the guests brought in from the "highways and hedges"—for Lk's readers, the Gentile mission of the church. Instead it is the people who have eaten the banquet who then issue invitations to others. Not only are the ones who only wanted a warm place and a good meal transformed into guests who want to share the celebration, they also become witnesses who carry on the mission of the church.

This modern version also struggles with the problem of a banquet that is ready now in a world where it seems that the kingdom has not come. On the one hand, the once-for-all event is important. The child's fifth birthday party is over and will never come again; it does not help to say that another will come next year. On the other, the host in this parable wants to have his banquet hall filled all the time, not just for one occasion.

At the end of the story we are left wondering. What does it mean to say, "We are at the party now"? Most of the time life does not seem to be a party, still less the kingdom banquet. Is that because we, like the guests who refused to come, are blind to what God offers us?

All With God At Table Are Sat Down

by Linda Strohmier

From: Luke 3:1-6, 22; Luke 14:15-24

Setting: The Seminary Chapel.

Characters:

The Very Important Person	Storyteller
Servant	Kid 1
Reggie Rockstar	Kid 2
Wanda Wall Street	Kid 3
Helen Household	Kid 4
Sam Student, Sandy Student	Kid 5
The Poor People	Kid 6
The Sick People	The Child
The Unhappy People	The Parents
The Children	
Johnny	
Mary	

Time: Right now.

Place: Right here.

[As the Gospel procession goes back into the sanctuary, the Story-Teller leads a group of kids (Kids 1-6) out of the Sacristy and processes (informally) with them to the Lectern. The StoryTeller (ST) opens the book to where "the story" is, and the kids sit down in front of the lectern (on the choir side). ST starts:]

ST: It's time for the story. Today I'm going to tell a story about a Very Important Person.

Kid 1: Is it my mother?

ST: Sort of.

Kid 2: Is it my dad?

ST: Sort of.

Kid 3: Is it a king?

ST: Sort of.

Kid 4: Is it the President?

ST: Well . . . [trying to stop questions and get on with the story]

Kid 5: Is it my teacher?

ST: [Trying again, but still trying to be nice . . .] Well, this Very Important Person—

Kid 6: I know! It's the Dean!

ST: [Riding over this. Wants to get on with the story.] This Very Important Person was the most important person you can think of. More important than your mother or your dad or a king or the President or your teacher — even more important than the Dean.

Kid 6: Nobody is more important than the Dean!

ST: This person was. This was the Very Most Important Super-Powerful Person you can think of, kind of like a king and the President and your teacher and your mom and dad and the Dean all rolled into one. This was a VERY IMPORTANT PERSON. Anyway, the Very Important Person decided to give a party.

Kid 1: What kind of party?

ST: The most wonderful kind of party you can imagine. Just exactly the kind of party a Very Important Person would give.

Kid 1: Was there stuff to eat?

ST: All kinds of wonderful stuff—

Kid 1: Ice cream?

Kid 2: And cake?

Kid 3: And spaghetti?

Kid 4: And Big Macs and french fries and pizza and cokes and chocolate milk shakes?

Kid 5: And peanut butter and jelly and candy—

Kid 6: And homemade pie like Ernest makes?

ST: All of that. Everything you can imagine that would make it the *best* party you can think of. [Trying to get on with it . . .] *Anyway*, the Very Important Person decided to give a party . . .

[At front of chapel, VIP enters, dressed however we think a VIP ought to dress. Followed by a Servant. The VIP is talking . . .]

VIP: [To Servant] I've decided that I'm going to give a big party.

Servant: Yes, ma'am. [Or Sir, whoever the VIP is . . .]

VIP: I'm going to give the biggest, the best party you can imagine.

Servant: Yes, ma'am.

VIP: It's going to be wonderful!

Servant: Of course, ma'am.

VIP: And I want you to invite all my friends. I could send them invitations in the mail, but this is Extra-Special. So I want you to go out, in person, and invite all my friends.

Servant: Yes, ma'am.

VIP: Tell them how much I want them to come to my party. And tell them there will be a *surprise!*

Servant: Yes, ma'am.

VIP: Now, let's see. Who all do I want to invite?

[VIP goes into consultation with the servant, walking around a bit, thinking, and adding names to a list.]

ST: Now the Very Important Person had *lots* of friends. Important people. Not as important as the Very Important Person, because nobody was as important as that, but important. So the Very Important Person thought and thought and made a list. [VIP writing list.] And then the Very Important Person sent the servant out to invite all the other important people, who were her friends.

[VIP finishes list, tells the Servant:]

VIP: Well, that's it. You go now and invite everybody on the list. And *I'll* go talk to the cooks about dinner.

[VIP exits to the sacristy; Servant reads the list, then starts out. The people she will meet are sitting at various places in the choir of the Chapel, probably on opposite sides of the two aisles between pews. They come out as she comes to them.]

ST: The first person on the list was Reggie Rockstar. The Very Important Person knew that Reggie loved parties, so he'd be sure to come.

[Servant meets Reggie at the first aisle. Reggie is combing his hair. Dressed *very* rockstar — lots of flashing colors, shiny fabrics.]

Servant: Mr. Rockstar! My boss, the Very Important Person, sent me to invite you to a party. She says it's going to be the best party you've ever been to and to be sure to come.

Reggie: Oh, no way! No way! I'm *so* busy! I have a concert at Madison Square Garden and then I'm going to Hollywood to make a movie and then my new book is coming out ... I couldn't come. No way! Tell her to ask me again next year.

Servant: But she asked you specially. She really wants you to come. And there's a surprise!

Reggie: Oh, no way! There aren't any surprises. Nothing could surprise me! Now run along. I have to work on my new album!

[Servant leaves Reggie, combing his hair. Then she meets Wanda Wall Street, across the center aisle.]

Servant: Ms. Wall Street, my boss, the Very Important Person, sent me to invite you to a party. She says it's going to be the best party you've ever been to and to be sure to come.

Wanda: [Very busy with papers, two telephones.] Oh, no I couldn't possibly come. I have business to do. I have a lot of big deals right now — a new oil well, and a gold mine, and the stock market is slipping, and tomorrow I have to meet with the President and the Senate. Oh, no, I couldn't possibly waste my valuable time on a party!

Servant: But she asked you specially. She really wants you to come. And there's a surprise!

Wanda: Oh, no, I simply can't fit it into my schedule. And anyway, I don't like surprises. We need to be able to plan ahead, to get everything in order. There's no place for surprises in this world! Run along. I have important business to do.

[Servant leaves Wanda, one telephone at each ear, papers and writing notes. At the next aisle she meets Helen Household, with two kids. Helen is very busy, ordering the kids around. The kids,

86

Johnny and Mary, are okay, just lively — like kids in Chapel are sometimes.]

Servant: Oh, Ms. Household. My boss, the Very Important Person, sent me to invite you to a party. She says it's going to be the best party you've ever been to, and to be sure to come.

Helen: Oh, I'd love to, but I just can't—

Johnny: Party? Party? I wanna go to the party!

Mary: Party? Can we go to the party?

Helen: Ssshhh. Quiet down! I'm talking! No, I just can't come. I have so much to do. I've got to get the laundry done, and the shopping—

Mary: Please, Mom, please!

Johnny: I want to go to the party!

Helen: I told you to be QUIET! Now, I've got a meeting at the church, and I've got to take a covered dish—

Mary: Oh, Mom!

Johnny: Please, Mom, please, let's go to the party!

Helen: Johnny! Mary! That's enough! SETTLE DOWN! Now we can't go to any party, and that's all there is to it. We have too many important things to do!

Servant: But she asked you specially. She really wants you to come. And there's a surprise.

Mary: A surprise? A surprise? Oh, come on, Mom, pleeeeeasssse.

Johnny: A surprise? A surprise? What is it, huh, what is it?

Servant: I can't tell you, but the Very Important Person wants you to come to the party and find out.

Helen: Well, we just can't and *that's it*! There just isn't any time. Maybe when the kids grow up . . . [To kids] Come on. Settle down and pay attention. You have to be *quiet* in Church!

[Servant goes on across the center aisle, to Sam and Sandy Student. Sam and Sandy are working away with a huge pile of books in front of them—notecards, papers, maybe even a typewriter . . .]

Servant: Oh, Mr. and Ms. Student. My boss, the Very Important Person, sent me to invite you to party. She says it's

going to be the best party you've ever been to and to be
sure to come.

Sam: Oh, I couldn't possibly. I've got a theology paper due
tomorrow—

Sandy: And I've got a liturgy exam—

Sam: And I've got to preach in my field parish on Sunday—

Sandy: And there's a worship committee meeting—

Sam: And spiritual direction—

Sandy: And the youth group—

Servant: But, Mr. and Ms. Student, my boss thought you'd be
sure to come to her party. She says you're always
talking and thinking and writing about the Very Important Person—and you're always saying that the Very
Important Person is your best friend. She thought sure
you'd come to her party!

Sandy: Oh, she matters to me a lot and I really hate to miss it,
but I've got all this work to do.

Sam: Yeah, GOE's are coming up and my commission—

Sandy: Tell her to have a party next summer.

Sam: Or next year, when I get out of seminary and have some
time . . .

Servant: But the party is *now*, and she really wants you to come.
There's a surprise.

Sandy: Oh, I can't take surprises *now*. I just *can't*.

Sam: Yeah, we really can't handle another thing right now. The
work we're doing is *much* too important.

Sandy: And my time schedule is too tight for surprises. Tell her
I'm sorry.

Sam: Yeah, maybe another time.

[They continue flipping through books, writing furiously,
shuffling cards and papers, maybe typing . . . Servant heads back
to the front of the chapel, toward the altar, very disappointed.]

ST: Well, the Servant had been to everybody on the list, and
nobody would come. They said they were all too busy.

[VIP enters from sacristy, with a plate and cup. Comes to front
of altar, greets the Servant.]

VIP: Oh, you're back! Is everybody coming?

ST: Oh, ma'am, I went to all your friends, and nobody can come. They're all too busy to come to a party.

VIP: Reggie Rockstar?

Servant: He has a concert and a movie . . .

VIP: Wanda Wall Street?

Servant: She says she has too much business. And anyway, she doesn't like surprises. She says you should plan things and there shouldn't *be* any surprises.

VIP: [Increasingly disappointed and upset] And Helen Household?

Servant: Well, Johnny and Mary wanted to come, but their Mom is too busy with laundry and shopping and the church meeting . . .

VIP: And Sam and Sandy Student? Surely *they*'ll come. They've been waiting for this party for years. They're always talking about it!

Servant: No, they have too many papers and sermons and exams and field work . . .

VIP: Well, what kind of friends are those? I'm giving the most important party ever—the very best party they could ever go to—and they're "too busy" to come. [Angry] And the party is all ready! There's ice cream and pizza and spaghetti and cake . . . [Has an idea] I tell you what! If my friends won't come, then you go and find people who *will*! You go ask everybody—anybody who's hungry or sick, people who are sad, people who don't *have* any friends to invite them to a party. You ask *them* to come to *my* party. *They*'ll be my friends! [VIP starts setting the table. Servant goes out into the Chapel, heads toward the back door.]

ST: So the Servant went out, to invite people to the best party of all. She went to Poor People, who had never been invited to a party by the important people . . .

[Servant meets a group of Poor People about halfway back in the choir.]

Servant: [To Poor People] Please come to a party. . .

Poor People: Who, us? Nobody wants us! Really? You want us to come to a party? Hurray!

[The Poor People start toward the altar.]

ST: So the Poor People hurried to come to the house of the Very
     Important Person. But there was still room. So the Servant
     went to the Sick People. . .
[Servant continues on, meets a group of Sick People (blind,
crippled, sick, etc.) toward the back of the choir.]
Servant: Please come to a party. . .
Sick People: You really want us? Nobody wants us.
Servant: The Very Important Person does.
Sick People: I already feel better. Let's go.
[The Sick People start toward the altar. Servant continues on.]
ST: And she went to Unhappy People.
[Servant meets Unhappy People, back in the rear section of the
Chapel.]
Servant: Please come to a party. . .
Unhappy People: Us? We don't have any friends to invite us to a
                 party.
Servant: The Very Important Person is your friend. She wants
          you to come to the party.
Unhappy People: Oh, wonderful! I feel so much happier!
[Unhappy People start toward the altar. Servant comes back to
the lectern.]
ST: And the Servant went to the children. . .
Servant: Please come to a party. . .
Children: Yay! Hurray! A grown-up party? Will there be pizza
           and ice cream and cake and spaghetti and McDonald's?
Servant: All the most wonderful things you can think of.
Johnny and Mary: [Coming out into aisle, leaving their mother.]
                  Us too?
Servant: You too. The Very Important Person wants *all* the
          children there especially. . .
All children: Hurray! Let's go!
[All the children in the Chapel head toward the Altar, bigger ones
leading littler ones. . . The Very Important Person is standing in
the chancel, in front of the altar, to welcome them.]
VIP: Welcome, welcome, everybody to my party! Y'all come,
      y'hear? Welcome, welcome!
[Everybody gathers around the altar, with special effort to have

some arranged at the communion rail, like people taking communion; others around in back, like the celebrants.]

VIP: Everybody, welcome to the party! I'm so glad you all would come and be my friends.

Everybody: Thank you, Very Important Person, thank you.

VIP: Now, everybody, I have a surprise for you. The reason I asked you here, to this very special party, is to announce a *big surprise*! This is a *birthday* party! This is my child, and it's his(her) birthday!

[From the back of the Chapel a couple enter, carrying a baby. They walk toward the front. As they come up the aisle, Reggie and Wanda and Helen and Sam and Sandy will join them. Servant starts saying, standing at the lectern:]

Servant: Prepare ye, prepare ye the way of the Lord! Make the paths straight! Make the mountains and valleys level! Make the crooked ways straight! Make the rough roads smooth! Look, everyone, and see! See the Lord! See the salvation of our God!

[At this announcement, the too-busy important people finally start to pay attention. As the couple with the baby come by, they come out and follow them to the altar.]

Reggie: Oh, I've got to come too.

Wanda: Oh, dear, I almost missed this!

Helen: Oh, this is important!

Sam and Sandy: Come on, the paper will just have to wait!

[All are now in procession, following the couple and baby to the altar. VIP is standing there in front of the altar, to receive them.]

VIP: Welcome, welcome to my house, everyone. Welcome to the most wonderful surprise of all. Welcome everyone. Welcome, all my friends. This is my child, and I want all of you to know him (her). This my beloved child, and I am very pleased with him (her).

Everyone: Hello, hello! Hurray! Hallelujah!

Cast and congregation join in a hymn.

At the end everybody takes a bow, and then goes back to their seats. Service continues with Prayers of the People.

Linda Strohmier's play is much changed from the parable in the versions we know. Like Mt and Lk, she has adapted it for her own setting and so changed it. The play is designed to be given in the Advent season; for this reason, it used both the parable and material from the beginning of Lk's gospel. It is to be presented in the context of a church service that includes Holy Communion, thus associating the kingdom banquet and the coming of the Christ child with the Eucharist. The setting is a seminary, and the play involves children who live in it. Thus it offers us an example of how the parable might be adapted for presentation in a variety of church situations.

The playwright has heard Jesus' emphasis that the kingdom is not what people ordinarily expect. Those who at first refuse to come to the party repeatedly express their antipathy to surprises, reminding us of the business-as-usual excuses of the guests in the parable. The surprise in the play is the coming of the Christ child. Are we to understand that the kingdom gift is the birth of Jesus? Or is the kingdom banquet the celebration of Holy Communion? The end of the play certainly suggests that it is. To make this association is to take a risk. The banquet of the kingdom, as Jesus spoke about it, is certainly not something to be reduced to a weekly religious ceremony—the way many of us think of Holy Communion—but perhaps the play calls us to see more in the community gathered around the Lord's table than we usually do. Is this the foretaste of the kingdom? Does it offer us the resources of the kingdom for living out our lives?

Finally, a striking note in the play is the fact that the original- ly invited guests decide at the last minute to come after all. Read- ing the play, we wish the child in the story before this one could have been part of the cast. She was so concerned about those guests who refused to come; we share her concern, and welcome the change. Gone is the note of judgment in the parable Jesus told. In its place we find inclusiveness—everyone is at the table. We do not forget the note of judgment in the other versions as we rejoice in this one.

The Party

by Sharon Chant

Claude gazed lovingly at the flickering light of the candle through his crystal goblet of fine old burgundy.

"Like rubies on fire," he thought, "so very brilliant and warm."

Life was very, very good to Claude. In the midst of war, with all Paris clutching its ration cards and praying to make it through another bitter winter of German occupation without starving, Claude lived in luxury in his elegant eighteenth-century town house in the corner of the Place des Vosges.

"Well," he had shrugged, "after all, one must be practical. One must deal with situations as they are. What's wrong with a little compromise if it keeps me in fine cigars and petrol? Life is too short to be a martyr."

A knock at the door interrupted Claude's after-dinner reverie. Shortly, the butler announced a messenger who was ushered into a drawing room lined with gilded boiserie. A soft Persian carpet and the luxurious furnishings contrasted sharply with the visitor's sad appearance. A shapeless corduroy coat hung from his bent choulders and he nervously turned the worn cap in his hands round and round.

"What is it you want?" Claude snapped, his left eyebrow arching in unspoken scorn.

"To invite you to a party, sir," the man answered quietly.

Claude's curiosity was aroused in spite of himself. Whom did he know who would send an invitation via such a disreputable-looking person? And a party in the midst of wartime?

"Who's giving this party?"

The name the man mentioned gave Claude a start; it was the man whose house this had been before the war, before the Germans had confiscated it.

"Why does he want me?" Claude asked the man suspiciously.

"He wants you to know that he does not blame you for what happened. He wants to have a chance to forgive you personally and to help you."

"Help me?! Help me!" Claude burst into sarcastic laughter. "How can he help me? I don't want his forgiveness and I certainly don't need his help."

"If you please, sir," the servant said more softly than before, "this will be a very wonderful party. I am told to tell you that you will not regret coming, only. . . ."

"Only what?" Claude shot back impatiently.

"Only, sir, you must come now, right away. My master said to tell you that all is now ready."

"What a curious man your master is to think that I would go out on a night like this on the spur of the moment. Doesn't he know who I am? I'm far too busy for this nonsense. Away with you!"

The messenger sighed in resignation and turned to go. The butler sneered as he held the door.

Upon his return home, a tall, aristocratic man in beautifully tailored but shabby clothes greeted him at the door.

"Well?" he asked urgently. "Is he coming?"

"No," answered the servant. "I tried to tell him, but he just wouldn't listen."

"The fool! Doesn't he realize his life is in danger?"

"I suppose not. It was hard to talk with the butler listening at the door, but I don't think he realizes that the Germans suspect him of underground activities. It's kind of ironic, you know, the poor devel thinks he's so safe because he goes along with them. He said he didn't need your help. If he only knew, eh, that you're the section-head of the Resistance for the whole Paris area!"

"Well, never mind that now. It's too late. Go and get the others and tell them the time has come."

The servant went back out into the cold crisp night and searched the dark narrow streets for the numbers he had been given.

"Mr. Rosenberg," he whispered as a sleepy man came to the door, "the Count wants you at his party. Please come with me now."

"Are you sure he wants me?" the man questioned cautiously.

"Yes, yes, please come right away."

The man quickly and quietly roused his family and, with what possessions they could carry, followed the servant.

"Mrs. Levy, the Count requests the honor of your company."

"Right now? Yes, I'm coming." The old lady trembled as she threw on her threadbare coat with the yellow star on the sleeve.

The servant made a few more stops before returning with a motley crew in tow.

"Here they are, sir," he announced proudly.

"Fine, fine," murmured the aristocrat, "but we still have some room on the plane and a little time left. Go find these others."

The servant returned in a little while with the two Polish families in the quarter, a young Hungarian girl who had fled her homeland, and three Belgian immigrants who worked by day in the porcelain factory and at night forging passports.

"Wonderful!" said the master. "Now we can leave."

The next morning the nets of the S.S. roundup were empty—empty, this is, with the exception of one very big, rich fish. The house on the Place des Vosges stood as a silent witness to the party of the night before.

Sharon Chant's offering is strikingly different from those we have seen. Paris under enemy occupation during World War II is a somber setting for a somber story, where life and death are literally at stake. We find an interesting echo of Jesus' parable here. Some of his listeners were surely offended that a wandering teacher with no credentials should dare to announce to them that the kingdom banquet was ready, that they were to come at once or be left out. So also the man in this story is insulted by the thought that his impoverished predecessor could be of help.

Here it is the host who saves—or can save, if the guest accepts his offer. The judgment theme present in Jesus' parable and so prominent in Mt's version is also featured here. The man who disdains the invitation brings judgment on himself, just as the man with the wrong garment did in Mt's parable.

We also do not miss the reversal that this story offers, in comparison with Mt's version. There is a strong note of hostility to Judaism in the story of Mt's king who destroys the city of his murderous guests. In the contemporary version, however, the guests who are saved are the Jews. Given the differences in the settings of the two stories, we cannot but believe that Mt would applaud this retelling of the parable.

Together the Day the Storm Hit

by Scott Dolph

Donovan got up. He had to get home soon because his mother expected him before dark. "The forest gets very dark at night, I don't want you to get lost," she would say.

As he got up from his favorite stump in the clearing beneath a spreading oak tree, he thought how nice this place was. He had been here many times before, and the place in all its beauty seemed like a home away from home. In fact the peacefulness of the place, and its quietness, made Donovan half wish it *were* a home away from home.

On the way up the dirt trail, stumbling along, Donovan thought of his friends at school. Soon it would be summer vacation and he would not see some of them until school started again the next year; Luke, who lived on the other side of town would probably not come to visit. This made Donovan sad, because Luke was his best friend: they played in the band together. Donovan played flute and Luke played piccolo. Together they played music that the other students either could not play or did not like. So Donovan wished he could be with Luke at least some of the summer, but knew his family would not like the idea. His friend was black.

At dinner Donovan got up the courage to mention how sad he was that school would soon be out. His father let out a snort of a laugh "When *I* was in school, we couldn't wait for summer vacation! What's the matter with you?"

Donovan stammered, "Uh, well, it's just that when school's out, I won't get to practice and play music with some of my friends. Really, I'm glad school's out . . . except for that."

"Now that's not so. Several of the band members live just

down the street. You know that," his mother answered. "It's those kids from the other side of town who won't be around. You'll be all right, wait and see."

Just after school the next day Donovan went again to the forest, to his favorite place. He sat down on that familiar stump. He began to daydream, and suddenly a little sparrow hopped close to him. When Donovan looked up the sparrow made a couple of chirps. Donovan was delighted. The bird began singing more heartily now, as if she were inviting him to stay. He could hardly believe what was happening! Who would believe it? After all, this was the first time after so many visits that one of the animals of the forest dared even to make its presence known. Now, the bird came right out and sang for Donovan to make him feel at home, like a good host.

It was about time to leave. Even with the lovely melodies, Donovan had to get back to the house. As he stood up, a small grey squirrel hustled up to him. Donovan was a bit startled, and looked back at the squirrel. There they stood, just staring at each other. Then the real show began. This creature was quite a musician in his own right. To Donovan's delight, the squirrel's chattering sounded to him like the madrigals he had heard in school from his teacher's record player. It was beautiful and flowing. Donovan had to stay for a few more minutes; to leave now would be an insult to the small performer! Then he got up and jogged back through the ruts and roots of the dirt trail he had traveled so often. But now something was different. This was no longer just a pleasant and quiet place to go, it had become a place where he had been invited to stay. It was a place where he felt welcome among creatures so different from each other, and from himself.

The next day was one that Donovan knew would come all too soon, the last day of school. Donovan had a plan, though; he knew he and Luke would be able to practice together. All he had to do now was to go talk to Luke and ask what his plans were for summer.

"Well, I don't know. I'll probably just hang out. Swim some. Maybe get a job if someone will hire me," Luke answered.

"How about practice?"

"Where? . . . I mean, your family won't let you come to my house, they already said no to you coming to my birthday party, *remember?*"

"But I've got just the place! It's in the forest. . ." Donovan then told Luke of the place and of his extraordinary experience there with the animals. "What do you think!"

"Let's go!"

Several days into the summer, Luke and Donovan met near their school and from there went up the street to the forest. With them, they carried their instruments and lunches. They were having such a good time getting to the special clearing, laughing and joking, singing and whistling, that they did not notice the huge thundercloud coming over the hill to the south. A clap of thunder. They looked at each other, scared. "We're too far from the house to get there before this thing hits us!"

They ran for shelter and huddled beneath the oak tree. The storm was sudden and violent.

As they sat, the cloud came overhead. The wind blew. Thunder crashed and lightning lit the sky with quick, sharp bursts. The rain began to fall: sprinkles at first, then torrents. Donovan's special place seemed completely different. The birds did not sing to welcome them; in fact, there were no birds around. The squirrels also hid. All that was familiar was the oak tree and the stump.

The boys were worried, but so far they had not gotten wet. The oak, with so many layers of branches above, sheltered them. As they sat together, waiting for the storm to pass Donovan said, "Seems like everyone—even Mother Nature—is trying to stop us from practicing!"

Luke nodded. Then, from where he sat, he looked over and what did he see, but a squirrel at the base of a nearby tree. Quietly, Luke pointed the creature out to Donovan.

Looking at the squirrel, Donovan was delighted; it was his friend, the madrigal squirrel! Even with the storm, Donovan pulled out his flute from its case and began to play. Luke followed by pulling out his piccolo. This time the squirrel was serenaded, instead of Donovan. He scampered into his nest. When he returned, other squirrels followed. Then the sparrow showed up, and with her came other birds. Before they knew it, Donovan and Luke were joined by a whole chorus there in the shelter of the spreading oak.

As quickly as it had come, the storm lifted and the cloud went over the next mountain. No one in the shelter of the oak noticed the storm was over until the sun came out, making the droplets of water on the tree's leaves glisten and glimmer like a crystal chandelier. The place was now more beautiful than Donovan had ever known it. It was pretty before, a place where he could go and be alone, but every time he came it got more familiar, more like home. And now he could share its beauty with his best friend. It was a place that was safe and welcoming for the two boys as outsiders. It was a place they did not make, but one that was given to them.

"I hate to say it, but it's getting dark. What d'you say we get a whole bunch of us to have a picnic here next week?" Luke suggested.

"Yeah!"

Scott Dolph's story does not refer explicitly to the Parable of the Great Feast. Read apart from the parable, it is a story about a boy who finds the right place for himself and for his friend, and then discovers that he is invited, welcomed, into it by those who were there before him. Read as a response to the parable, that is, as a story about the kingdom, there is more to it than first meets the eye. The hosts, a sparrow and a squirrel, are as unlikely as some of Jesus' images of the kingdom—the mustard seed, the leaven. In this refuge there is both freedom and community. The storm is severe, but it does not touch anyone here. At the end it is Luke, whom Donovan has brought in, who suggests including others. The community continues to expand. Will there finally be so many children that the birds and animals will be driven away? Not in this magic place. Here the hosts will continue to be hosts and to welcome those who come.

Is the kingdom a refuge, a quiet place away from the world? Of course it is not. The kingdom, this story suggests, is the experiences of wholeness that sometimes come upon us as gifts and remind us that business-as-usual, with its struggle and brokenness, is not the truth about life. We are offered wholeness and community.

Many of the issues raised in Jesus' parable, and in Mt's and Lk's versions of it, have been echoed and developed in these five pieces. Each one enriches the conversation. Yet a major question raised by the parable for twentieth-century Christians and not directly addressed so far is, how does God exercise power in our world today?

For we have heard that the kingdom of God is about God's exercise of power in the world, and not simply about an interior reality in each of us, and not only a hope for a far-off, future reality. We have heard Jesus say, "Come, for all is now ready." We have noticed that for Jesus and Mt and Lk the kingdom is not an individual experience, either in this world or after death in another world. On the contrary, it is a reality shared by all who come together at Jesus' call, the gathered community of anyone who will come.

We have also learned that participation in the kingdom imposes some terms on those would come. The first condition is simply that we do come, that we answer the invitation and that we answer it now. But there are other terms, too. Jesus suggests that one of the conditions is that we sit down and eat (share our lives) with the others who come, no matter who they turn out to be. Mt and Lk, each in different ways, suggest further conditions. To live out the righteousness God has given us is a dominant note in Mt; to treat the poor and unfortunate as the ones who come into the kingdom first is Lk's message, as well as his reminder that we must continue to carry out the mission of the church by calling others.

Since the parable, indeed, the Gospels, have been part of our lives for a long time, much of this is old stuff for us. We have seen

how the parable functioned for Jesus and Mt and Lk, how it challenged their listeners and upset their usual assumptions about life
and the world. Does the parable work that way for us? In our
better moments we yearn to be challenged out of our routine
thinking and our business-as-usual lives. We would really love to
be surprised by God's exercise of power in the world as we know
it, and we want to share God's reign deeply with others. The
parable seems to promise us such a reality and call us into it.
Is it true? Is it possible? Or is it only a reality we long for as we
go about the normal business of doing the best we can?

I do not have a spectacular, dramatic answer to these questions. I offer only a suggestion or two in the hope of persuading
others to join the conversation.

If what Jesus said in this parable is true, then a good deal of
what the world tells us and we tell each other is a lie. We usually
think that we know how power is exercised in the world, whether
it is in the political arena, or the economic, or the religious, or the
individual and personal. Whether we ourselves wield power or are
powerless, we think we know how things work and who is in
charge. The parable claims that God is in charge.

We believe that nothing new or unexpected happens. We tell
each other that the more things change, the more they stay the
same. In the face of constant change, we say that everything
changes but nothing gets better. There is truly an enormous
amount of evidence to support such attitudes: tragedy, personal
and global, is everywhere. The predictability of things, people,
events, and institutions is a monotonous reality. The parable
claims that we can expect the unexpected.

God's exercise of power in the world is unexpected and full
of surprises. Since we do not expect the unexpected, we may
miss what God offers. Since we do not like or want surprises, we
may domesticate events, reinterpret them to suit our ways of
thinking. Events are not self-explanatory. When we interpret
them to ourselves, we may drain them of power in order to
maintain our precarious control of things. God may be active
in ways we fail to discern—among people, communities, and
nations. Mt suggests that God was active in the Roman destruction of Jerusalem; we do not have to agree with his interpretation

to consider the possibility that God has a hand in the affairs of nations. Among communities of all kinds there are events to celebrate, moments when life breaks free of oppression and offers new possibilities. Many of these may go unnoticed and their potential be missed because we believe the lies we tell each other, and do not believe that God really makes a difference. God's reign may be making inroads in this dreary old world, in ways we fail to discern or act on.

To what are we called by God, who exercises power in the world? We are surely called, together, to watch. In the gospels Jesus repeatedly tells his disciples to watch. Watch for what? We are to watch not merely for the triumphant coming again of Jesus, but also for events that signify God's exercise of power. We need to watch together because none of us is able to see alone and interpret alone. We need to work on interpretations, and check ours against those of others, and learn from each other. Those "others" need to be people unlike ourselves, people as dissimilar as that motley crew that Jesus pictured coming into the feast, from whom we will learn the significance of events by listening to them tell us how they see things. It is especially important to listen to the marginal people in our society, not because they are better than we are but because their angle of vision allows them to see things that others do not. Lk's insistence that the poor and marginal be brought into the feast first may mean that they have something to say about the exercise of God's power in the world that we will not hear from anyone else.

Watching for God's exercise of power and listening to each other as we try to interpret it will not bring unanimity, but differences of conviction. People will diverge widely in their convictions about what we must do in order to be faithful to God's activity. Because we want consensus and not diversity, we will get discouraged all over again.

Discouragement comes because we persist in believing that we are in charge. Were we to take seriously the claim that God is in charge, we would be free to grasp the opportunities for new life that are offered. When people do this together, the world can be changed. We might even be able to hear Mt as he tells us that we can live out the righteousness that God has given us. We are not fated to be the man with the wrong garment at the banquet. Living out the righteousness given us by God might not only be possible, but turn out to be much more interesting and challenging than counting our sins or the shortcomings of others.

Lk insists on the mission of the church. One thing this mission might mean is that we are called to watch for God's action in the world, and participate in what God is doing so that others can see and join in. To do this will not solve all the problems, nor will it bring in the full, visible kingdom of God. That should come as no surprise. To watch for God's action in the world will not transform everything, but it might just transform us and those with us who will accept the unexpected invitation to the party.

The Second Invited

by Elizabeth Hooper

Really?
Even me?
Just as I am?
Oh, but I couldn't!
I'd like to, though.
Come immediately? I will.
Exactly as I am.

103

SUGGESTED BIBLIOGRAPHY

Of the literally hundreds of books about Jesus
and the gospels, the following may be especially helpful:

Paul Achtemeier, *The Inspiration of Scripture* (Philadelphia: Westminster Press, 1980).
Hans Conzelmann, *A History of Primitive Christianity* (Nashville: Abingdon, 1973).
John Dominic Crossan, *In Parables* (New York: Harper & Row, 1973).
Frederick W. Danker, *Luke* (Philadelphia: Fortress Press, 1976).
O.C. Edwards, *Luke's Story of Jesus* (Philadelphia: Fortress Press, 1981).
Reginald H. Fuller, *A Critical Introduction to the New Testament* (London: Duckworth, 1966).
Reginald H. Fuller, *Interpreting the Miracles* (Philadelphia: Westminster, 1963).
Joachim Jeremias, *Rediscovering the Parables* (New York: Scribner's, 1966).
Werner H. Kelber, *Mark's Story of Jesus* (Philadelphia: Fortress Press, 1979).
Jack Dean Kingbury, *Matthew* (Philadelphia: Fortress Press, 1979).
John Koenig, *Jews and Christians in Dialogue* (Philadelphia: Westminster Press, 1979).
Norman Perrin, *Rediscovering the Teaching of Jesus* (New York: Harper & Row, 1967).
Norman Perrin, *The New Testament: An Introduction* (New York: Harcourt, Brace, 1974).

In addition, readers are urged to become acquainted with *The Interpreter's Dictionary of the Bible*, which contains articles listed alphabetically by subject on virtually everything related to Bible study.

Cowley Publications is a work of the Society of St. John the Evangelist, a religious community for men in the Episcopal Church. The books we publish are a significant part of our ministry, together with the work of preaching, spiritual direction, and hospitality. Our aim is to provide books that will enrich their readers' religious experience and challenge it with fresh approaches to religious concerns.